What Readers Are Saying About Jay Payleitner's Books

52 Things Daughters Need from Their Dads

"My little girl is almost two and your book really put things in perspective... It makes you look at who you are, who you should be, and who you want your daughter to see."

—Mark, Illinois

"Two little girls, 10 and 8. I have been thanking God every day for the past week since I saw your book in the airport. Completely inspirational and has driven me to recommit to myself and my family to be a thoughtful and caring presence in their lives."

—Jim, New York

"Your book was very touching. I think I even wept at the first few chapters. I am a father to a seven-month-old special girl, and I think it is impossible to do it without God's help. We are on a mission!"

—Kok Siang, Singapore

52 Things Kids Need from a Dad

"Your book has inspired me to try harder with my sons and give to them time and wisdom my dad (who wasn't around except for holidays) was unable to give to me."

—John, Oregon

"I've highlighted and put notes all over the book, and it's definitely one of my favorites."

—Aaron, Virginia

"I have been searching for such a book I can give to my son-in-law as he and my daughter await the birth of their first child...and depending on whether my grandchild is a boy or girl, there may be another book of yours in his future as well!"

—Bill, California

52 Things Wives Need from Their Husbands

"Reading your book was a great reminder of simple things I can do to be intentional on a regular basis."

—Alem, Illinois

52 Things Husbands Need from Their Wives

"This book is definitely helping me in my marriage as well as my household... For every wife struggling and wondering what's going on in that big head of our husband, I want to say thank you...for your insight, your knowledge, and your suggestions!"

—Keisha, North Carolina

52 Things Wives Need from Their Husbands
52 Things Husbands Need from Their Wives

"My husband and I are reading these books together, and it has been so much fun! I love your style of writing. And your words of wisdom have helped me to focus on some things in my marriage I haven't given much thought to for a long time, if ever. You are my new favorite author! Keep up the good work.

—Rachelle, Wisconsin

"Thank you for taking the time to share in such a lighthearted, humorous way. Your insights helped us see things from a different perspective. Marriage can be challenging but it is a treasure we must protect."

—Crystal, Illinois

10 Conversations Kids Need to Have with Their Dad

Jay Payleitner

HARVEST HOUSE PUBLISHERS
EUGENE, OREGON

Cover by Left Coast Design, Portland, Oregon

Cover photo © i love images / Cultura / Getty Images

Jay Payleitner is represented by the Steve Laube Agency, 5025 N. Central Ave., #635, Phoenix, AZ 85012-1502.

10 CONVERSATIONS KIDS NEED TO HAVE WITH THEIR DAD
Copyright © 2014 by Jay Payleitner
Published by Harvest House Publishers
Eugene, Oregon 97402
www.harvesthousepublishers.com

ISBN 978-0-7369-6031-1 (pbk.)
ISBN 978-0-7369-6032-8 (eBook)

Library of Congress Cataloging-in-Publication Data
    Payleitner, Jay K.
    10 conversations kids need to have with their dad / Jay Payleitner.
        pages cm
    ISBN 978-0-7369-6031-1 (pbk.)
    1. Child rearing—Religious aspects—Christianity. 2. Parenting—Religious aspects—Christianity. 3. Fatherhood—Religious aspects—Christianity. 4. Conduct of life. 5. Christian life. I. Title. II. Title: Ten conversations kids need to have with their dad.
    BV4529.17.P383 2014
    248.8'421—dc23

                                                              2014006766

Printed in the United States of America

14 15 16 17 18 19 20 21 22 / BP-CD / 10 9 8 7 6 5 4 3 2 1

To my brother, Mark,
in gratitude for the many years of bunk bed conversations

Contents

The Case for Questions

by Bob Tiede

I have six remarkable grandkids. And they all love to jump into Papa's arms for giant hugs. But with my youngest granddaughter, Clare, it wasn't always that way. When she was three or four, some shyness crept in, and Clare kept her distance.

Finally, during one visit, I gently said, "Clare, can I ask you some *tough* questions?" Those words drew her in. Her inquisitive nature prevailed. Like most kids, when a grown-up showed genuine interest in her opinion, Clare was eager to share.

My questions that day were not exactly puzzlers. "Clare, what's your favorite color?" "Which do you think runs faster, a bunny or a frog?" But the ice was broken. Three years later, every time she sees her Papa she joyfully expects a fresh batch of questions. Some thought-provoking, some silly.

My rewarding experience with Clare came to mind when I reviewed this book by my friend Jay Payleitner. He and I go way back. We worked together for more than a decade on *Josh McDowell Radio*. The parenting strategies that came up in the recording studio with Josh and co-host Wayne Shepherd hit close to home. Many have also found their way into the pages you're about to read.

Jay recommends two proven strategies for loving, leading, and dialoguing with your kids: *Telling stories. Asking questions.* To his credit, Jay is borrowing those parenting and leadership tactics from the greatest communicator in history: Jesus of Nazareth.

Consider the Prodigal Son, the Lost Sheep, the Four Soils, and the Good Samaritan. Jesus used parables to provide clear pictures of the attributes of God and how we should live as members of God's family. Earthly fathers can do the same thing.

Even better than story-telling is question-asking. The Bible documents more than 150 questions asked by Jesus. Can you imagine his voice?

> "Show me a Roman coin. Whose picture and title are stamped on it?" (Luke 20:24 NLT).

> "Which of these three do you think was a neighbor to the man who fell into the hands of robbers?" (Luke 10:36).

> "Do you love me?" (John 21:17).

> "What is written in the Law?…How do you read it?" (Luke 10:26).

> "Simon, are you asleep? Couldn't you watch with me even one hour?" (Mark 14:37 NLT).

These questions stopped the disciples and others in their tracks. They were forced to think and respond. In the same way, a father is much more likely to engage his son or daughter by asking a question than by lecturing or barking orders.

I wholeheartedly endorse this book. Jay's light touch and winsome style will help focus your own convictions and encourage you to initiate some of those vexing conversations we all need to have with our kids.

Best of all, sprinkled throughout the book are challenging questions I can ask Clare and all my grandkids for years to come.

Bob Tiede
CRU Director of Global Operation Leadership Development
leadingwithquestions.com

A QUIZ:

Are You and Your Kids Communicating?

1. Does your child spend more time texting with friends than talking to you? Even when you are in the same room, at the same table, or in the same car?

2. Do you get one-word answers to most of your questions? Words like "fine," "okay," "later," "no," or "whatever"?

3. When your kids come home, do they go their separate ways? Hiding in their rooms? Buried in video games, smartphones, or other digital technology?

4. Do you know what your kid has planned for this weekend? This summer?

5. Do you know what your kid is considering for college or a career?

6. Can you name your child's best friend? Worst enemy?

7. Which of their hobbies, sports, and extracurricular activities do they really, really love? And which are they doing for you?

8. Is your kid making good, thoughtful decisions?

9. When you tell them about a mandatory family event happening in the next 48 hours, are they surprised even though you've been talking about it for a month?

10. Has your child ever taught you something?

11. Does it feel like there's an invisible force field that prevents you from entering their bedroom?

12. Do you have a toddler or youngster and desperately want to lay the groundwork for years of fantastic conversations?

Dad, don't bother scoring this quiz. We both already know the results.

Things Need to Be Said

From you to them. From them to you. There is much give-and-take to be given and taken.

And saying what needs to be said is going to take actual spoken words.

Which is actually very good news! Conversations with your kids are one of the great privileges of being a dad. They can be fun, rewarding, and empowering.

Without conversation, ideas will never be exchanged. Fears and frustrations will never be uncovered. Your wisdom and experience will remain untapped and wasted. You will never fully appreciate your child's fresh vision nor get a chance to help focus their unique energy.

Dare I say it? The best opportunity your children have to reach their God-given potential begins with you, Dad. And that requires the ability to converse.

Your three-part plan includes

1. entering their world

2. earning the right to be heard

3. clarifying your own perspective

Entering their world

If you live, play, eat, and exist in separate worlds, critical conversations will never take place.

Entering their world is easy when they're little. Young kids will make time for you and fit into your schedule. But as they get older, you need to make time for them. You need to intentionally create environments and situations that bring you face-to-face or side by side. Working. Traveling. Playing. Goofing. Competing. Gardening. Woodworking. Barbecuing. Stargazing. Dancing. Dining. Going out for ice cream. Strolling a beach. Shopping for a Mother's Day present. Or serving dinner in a homeless shelter. You get the idea.

The best conversations don't happen after you say, "We need to talk." The best conversations with your son or daughter happen when you're *doing*. Maybe doing something for him, for her, for yourself, for a neighbor, for a friend, or even for God.

What's more, don't expect your kids to embrace all the great truths and core values in a single conversation. Handing down life skills is a way of life. It requires daily relationship. The Bible teaches that parents should pass on truths during our routine existence:

> These commandments that I give you today are to be on your hearts. Impress them on your children. Talk about them when you sit at home and when you walk along the road, when you lie down and when you get up (Deuteronomy 6:6-7).

Dad, feel free to interpret that passage loosely to suggest, "Talk to your kids about stuff that matters during TV commercials, riding in the car, strolling down a dirt road, when you're tucking them in bed, or at your favorite diner munching on blueberry waffles."

Consider for a moment the world your son or daughter has created. Their bedroom, their circle of friends, their teams and clubs, their safe zone, their "aura." Where and how can you enter that world? And how can you make sure they will be glad you're there? That's the goal.

Earning the right to be heard

The life-changing conversations you want to have with your kids will never happen if they don't respect you.

You can't demand respect, Dad—you can only earn it. The title of "father" doesn't automatically mean your kids will listen to you. Sure, they'll give you a chance. Up through the age of seven or eight they will give you plenty of opportunities to prove yourself to be reliable, compassionate, and trustworthy. After that, it gets harder.

Way too many dads lose their kids' respect. If you have a history of verbally trashing them or physically abusing them, what makes you think they will listen to anything you have to say? They won't. Also, if you let them walk all over you and you never follow through on discipline, they will see you as a pushover with no power or authority.

Thankfully, the opposite is also true. If your verbal interaction is affirming and if your touch is always under control, then you will be trustworthy. If you speak truth and listen to their side of the story before judging, then your word has value. If you respond calmly and consistently to their tantrums, pouting, or whining, they will acknowledge you as a peacekeeper. If you listen to their fears and dreams without derision, they will ask for your wisdom and experience with confidence.

If you're just realizing that you may have lost some of your children's respect, you have some extra work to do. Begin today. Start with delivering your own heartfelt doses of love and respect.

How do kids respond to a father they respect? With obedience, affection, attention to what you have to say, confidence you will do your best, and trust that you will supply their needs.

Best of all, they will put down their phones, turn off the TV, take out their earbuds, or stop texting long enough to hold a real conversation.

Clarifying your own perspective

The following ten chapters cover more than just how to have more verbal interaction with your kids. That's actually pretty easy:

- Spend more time with them
- Find common interests
- Listen
- Ask questions
- Be agreeable more than disagreeable

You knew all that, right? It's called getting along. These are skills you use all the time in adult conversations. In business, friendships, romantic relationships, and interacting with the neighbors. It's how you exchange information.

Certainly, these pages will expand on ways to open doors of communication with your children. But once those doors are open, what do you say and how do you say it?

We've got you covered. Whether they admit it or not, your kids are counting on you for guidance. They're making discoveries and decisions every day and you're the right person to help them sort out right from wrong, safe from dangerous, and better from best.

Much of what you want to say is already crystal clear in your head. You just need to find the right conversational openings in the course of daily life. On some of these issues, you could use a little help filling in some strategic gaps. That's why these chapters include some verifiable research, some perspectives from an older dad, and some fresh ideas to deliver old truths. You'll be glad to know the book also covers some issues you haven't yet had a chance to think through completely.

Dad, you've come to the right place. For the most part, you'll be nodding your head at just about everything you're about to read. But if something doesn't hit you quite right, that's not a problem. You're the dad. You're a critical gatekeeper for what enters their spongelike brains. My goal is to encourage you to walk confidently alongside your kids on the road of life, well-prepared to prepare them well.

There are things that need to be said. Ready, Dad?

On Family

"There is no doubt that it is around the family and the home that all the greatest virtues, the most dominating virtues of human society, are created, strengthened, and maintained."

Winston Churchill

"When I was a boy of fourteen, my father was so ignorant I could hardly stand to have the old man around. But when I got to be twenty-one, I was astonished by how much he'd learned in seven years."

Mark Twain

Let's begin this book on conversations with the story of a conversation that didn't take place.

The year is 2008. My son Randall proposed to a delightful young lady named Rachel. She said yes. And plans began for an early autumn wedding. My wife, Rita, and I, along with Randall's three brothers, were joyously looking forward to a wonderful addition to the family. Our daughter, Rae Anne, not so much.

Rae Anne, 15 at the time, was secretly resentful of the idea that an outsider would be breaking up her gang. She liked having four brothers. She liked being the only girl. And she didn't want anyone messing with the chemistry of her family. That feeling really had nothing to do with Rachel. To Rae Anne's credit, there wasn't an emotional display of cattiness or meanness. There was no confrontation or showdown.

My daughter was smart enough to never say or do anything she would regret later.

The outdoor October wedding was beautiful. Rae Anne was an elegant bridesmaid, and in the months that followed a miraculous thing happened. Rae saw that instead of breaking up the family, the addition of a sister-in-law actually made the Payleitners stronger. For the first time, Rae Anne had a big sister. It really didn't take long before my daughter and daughter-in-law became the best of friends, seeking each other's company even when no other Payleitner was present.

Dad here—who had been oblivious to the entire summer of one-sided animosity—was totally surprised when the truth came out. As we sat around our kitchen table one Sunday afternoon not long ago, Rae Anne admitted, "Oh yeah, I hated Rachel for about a year." Others at the table were rather amused, but I was stunned.

I had always been the kind of dad who knew what was going on. Or so I thought. My door was always open to talk through problems and concerns. I worked hard—sometimes biting my tongue—to listen to my kids without judgment until all the facts were on the table. But I had totally missed a yearlong grudge held by my daughter living right under my roof.

So why did Rae Anne and I not have a conversation? In my mind, a ten-minute chat would have soothed my daughter's concerns and put her heart at ease. Isn't that what daddies do? We make everything better, right? But then again, sometimes our kids don't come to us. Or can't. Or won't. And maybe there's nothing I could have said that would have convinced my daughter that everything was going to work just fine.

So what's the lesson? I can think of several.

First, dads don't know everything a daughter or son might be thinking. Second, even if we think we're in the loop, we might not be. Also, dads can't fix everything. And dads especially can't fix things we don't know about.

On the plus side, it all worked out. In the end, the story has become another part of Payleitner family lore. And, remember that the episode *did* include a very amusing and rewarding conversation. The one at the kitchen table where Rae Anne confessed her yearlong grudge. If it had been up to me, that revealing conversation could have taken place much earlier. But, as you know, Dad, it's not always up to us. And all we can do is give our best.

Conversations hold a family together

Sometimes conversations just happen spontaneously. But an intentional nudge by a perceptive father can create conversation-friendly environments throughout the course of day, week, year, or life.

An occasional one-on-one, heart-to-heart dialogue at an ice-cream parlor, on a hiking path, or during a long car ride can help a child anchor themselves to loving parents. Include lots of love, laughter, and dream-sharing.

A boisterous debate around a dinner table can sharpen wits and ward off lazy thinking. If everyone stays respectful, even a few reasonable disagreements can bond the generations. The goal is not hurt feelings, but engaged interaction.

Memories and tall tales shared around a crackling campfire settle nicely in the corners of your children's minds. I think it has something to do with the chemical reaction when you mix marshmallows, graham crackers, and Hershey bars.

Visits back home or to retirement homes should include open-ended questions that lead grandparents or great-grandparents to share lifelong memories. Too often those times together include way too much talk about the weather, today's news headlines, or their latest physical ailments. No wonder your kids are bored. Keep asking questions until your father or grandfather tells a story or two that even you have never heard before. Don't delay. Those memories fade when you least expect it.

Planning family vacations, birthday bashes, baby showers, and graduation parties shouldn't happen in a vacuum. Sure someone has to be in charge, but let those occasions be an excuse to get together in the weeks leading up to and following the gathering. Big events are a blur.

Ofttimes, the most fun is found in the planning before and memory sharing after.

A dad taking a few quiet minutes before bedtime prayers to retrace the day can uncover experiences that might otherwise remain unsaid. That includes good stuff like praise from a teacher or a funny text from a friend. And bad stuff that dads need to know about like hurt feelings, an encounter with a bully, or not-so-nice words either spoken or heard. While tucking in, Dad can help put the events of the day in perspective, so the next day can start with no regrets.

It's hard to put into words the importance of words.

When it comes to family, the ability to talk is just as important as what you talk about. Sure, you want to cover the big issues: hopes, dreams, spiritual truths, moral values, sexual purity, money, and eternity. Many of those ideas are covered in later chapters. But you can't have life-changing talks unless you also have slice-of-life talks: where the sun goes at night, how cat whiskers work, why ants sometimes travel in straight lines and sometimes scatter, what causes brain freeze when you drink a slushie too fast.

The issue of big talks versus impromptu talks is similar to the debate between quality time and quantity time. You never know when "big talks" and "quality time" are magically going to happen. You really can't expect an announcement from your son or daughter that says, "The next 20 minutes is critical to our relationship and my maturity." So, you have to put in the time and do the chit-chat. Those breakthrough moments will naturally come.

That doesn't mean the small moments need to be painful. Just the opposite! Dads should embrace the goofing-around part of fatherhood. Lying in the grass and pointing out shapes in the clouds. Middle school science-fair projects in which you do 49 percent of the work. Carpooling to a church youth event with an SUV full of weirdly dressed middle schoolers. Cartwheels and cannonballs. Riddles and rhymes. Library whispers and canyon echoes.

Celebrate those short and silly conversations and they will overflow into longer, deeper talks that impact your son or daughter forever.

In strong families

…you make time for each other.

…you circle the wagons and defend each other during
*   tough times.*

…members apologize easily and don't hold grudges.

…traditions are respected.

Talking traditions

Do you want to get your teenager talking? Easy. Simply make a change in a family tradition.

Don't serve cranberries at Thanksgiving. Cancel the annual drive to see Christmas lights because the weather's bad. Put a new angel or star on top of the tree. When they notice—and they will—expect to hear urgent demands such as, "We have to!" and "We've always done it that way!"

Funny though, the very next holiday, when you gather for some other tradition, that same teenager will do just the opposite. In a mocking tone they'll say, "Omigosh, that is so lame. I can't believe you still expect us to do that."

I suggest you don't confront your teen about their ever-changing perspectives. That's a no-win situation. Instead, look at that attribute as endearing. Stuck between childhood freedom and adult responsibility, young people crave traditions to give them stability and roots. At the same time, they are also trying out their sprouting wings. Every day brings new discoveries and new options. From a father's perspective, it's an amazing, jaw-clenching, and fulfilling process to watch.

I don't usually recommend that parents give in to teenage demands, but this may be the exception. When they insist on keeping a tradition, absolutely agree with them. Share some memories about when that tradition began and how it evolved from something your family happened to do into something you had to do.

Also, when they suggest abandoning a tradition in favor of a new way of doing things, again, absolutely follow their lead. The ensuing conversation may still include a little family history, but encourage your teenager to explain why new is better.

Holding tight to traditions

One game worth playing with your kids is to remember and make a list of traditions. When I start doing that, I get a little melancholy. The list would be long and would include backyard campfires, Thanksgiving football, Independence Day fireworks at the local golf course, multiple deliveries of Peeps from multiple kids to my wife at Easter, Christmas stockings hung by the chimney with care, a family movie outing between Christmas and New Year, driveway stickball, calling shotgun, and texting Mom when you get to your destination safely. All those we pretty much still do.

But there are quite a few traditions we've let slide for one reason or another. As tightly as dads want to hold on to most traditions, perhaps it's equally as important to be able to let them go. Kids get older. Homes are bought and sold. Family members pass on. New family members bring their own traditions. Sometimes tragedy or loss leads to change. Often, it's just time and circumstance.

I deeply cherish the memories of 14 years of Christmas skits—featuring 11 cousins—conceived, written, and produced mostly by my oldest son, Alec, but then passed on to his younger siblings one at a time.

For 30 years, until 1978, three generations of Payleitners went to the same big cottage on Pine Lake in Wisconsin for a week each summer. But it just didn't make sense after Grandpa died.

For 20 years, we dragged our kids to a department store for photos with Santa Claus. The tradition begins with baby Alec in 1980, but flipping through the photo album, a new sibling joins him in '83, '86, '88, and '93. For some reason, Alec just didn't want to sit on Santa's lap after he turned 21 and that's where the photo album ends.

Also coinciding with the years our kids were little was the famous Payleitner Easter-egg hunt. At its peak we were welcoming more than

50 kids plus their parents, filling more than 750 plastic eggs, and orchestrating a backyard event that was part celebration and part outreach.

Holding tightly to traditions in the moment sets the stage to hold them loosely enough to know when to let them go. No guilt or remorse. Sometimes the looser you hold on to something, the more easily it can evolve into something new and even more meaningful.

Some of our favorite traditions, I'm sure, we'll bring back when the time is right. As of this writing, Rita and I have one grandson. And we're expecting a few more grandkids in the next decade. You can be sure that Jackson and his cousins will have several seasonal and holiday traditions to hang on to forever. Some might be all-new, but most of them will be carried over from the "old days" of their mommies and daddies.

Triggering traditions

It's worth noting that conversations don't trigger traditions. It's actually the other way around. Traditions get family members talking: "Remember this"; "Don't forget that"; "This summer let's make sure…"; and "I'm going to be late this year, so someone else is going to have to…" Once you start hearing those conversations, Dad, you can just sit back and watch the memory-making unfold.

Beyond scheduled traditions, there's an entire array of traditions that are not on your family calendar, but happen anyway. You don't even have to think about them and they require zero preparation. But you know the triggers:

The first nice weekend of summer triggers a family bike ride.

The first snowfall of the year that is "good packing" triggers a family snowman contest.

The local high school presents their annual musical, so you order tickets for the Sunday matinee.

Shamrock Shakes come out at McDonald's, so you make a family dessert run.

The church across town holds their "live Nativity scene," so you bundle up the kids and go.

The zoo announces a new baby giraffe or lion cub, which means your family will be one of the first in line to see the little cutie.

As hard as you might try, I'm not sure you can orchestrate these kinds of family traditions. They evolve spontaneously. So be warned. To a kid, if you do something just twice, they expect it to become a regular, time-honored, unwritten law set in stone. As my daughter, Rae Anne, said years ago when insisting we stop for cones at an ice-cream store near the bike trail, "We have to stop here. It's a tradition!" And, you know what? She was right.

What are yours?

Have you and your kids had a chance to identify your family traditions? You may not call them such, but that's what they are, and they are enormously important. The ones around the holidays are easier to identify. But maybe this list might help jog your memory.

Do you stop for ice cream, donuts, or slushies after or before certain events?

Do you sit in the same pew at church?

Do you have a favorite museum, zoo, arboretum, park, or pool?

Do you see certain cousins or other extended family members annually?

In the car, are there silly family traditions when you pass specific landmarks?

Do you pose for photos at certain locations (like scenic overlooks) or events (like the first day of school)?

Do you have any traditions in the car, at the library, on vacations, or before bedtime?

Traditions define a family. And Dad, I recommend you crown yourself "Official Keeper of Traditions." If you accept that role, you'll establish yourself as trustworthy and consistent. Your children will honor you and follow your lead because they have come to rely on you day after day, year after year.

One of the expectations of church elders, outlined in 1 Timothy 3:4, is that an elder "must manage his own family well, having children who respect and obey him" (NLT). Keeping traditions is a part of managing your family and raising children who are on the same page as you—respectful and obedient.

Between the turkey and pumpkin pie

One of my favorite family traditions deserves a special mention. I recommend it wholeheartedly. At Thanksgiving, don't allow your family to race away from the table to watch football or rush to Black Friday sales that are, sadly, starting earlier and earlier. So much effort was put into preparing the meal and getting the family assembled, it's disrespectful to the cook and the host. Instead, stay seated for a while, let the meal digest, and enjoy the company.

For years, the Payleitner family has intentionally held off dessert for an hour or so. We pass around a basket with preprinted questions. Everyone gets a turn, and you never know what question you're going to get. Over the years, we've heard some surprising responses to simple questions.

"What's your earliest memory?" led my grandmother, who was born in 1900, to recall the sunny afternoon she was hanging laundry as a young teenager and was amazed when an airplane flew overhead. She had heard about those flying contraptions, but had never seen one before.

"What do you want to be doing ten years from now?" led one of my children to reveal some substantial life plans that no one at the table had ever heard before. It was a memorable moment.

"What's the scariest thing that ever happened to you?" led to my mom revealing the story of how—back in 1944—she broke off her engagement with a guy who didn't take the news very well. He threatened and stalked her for several days, until her brothers stepped in. Her story was gripping. She would meet my father a year later.

"Name a great challenge you have overcome" led Max to tell the story of how he blew out his knee in a varsity football game and required major surgery. The doctor laid out an aggressive rehab schedule and told Max he would be lucky to play baseball that spring. But Max posted a note on his bedroom wall that said, "JANUARY 18—GET IT DONE." He surprised everyone and came back midway through

the wrestling season to win 14 straight matches and earn a trip to the state finals.

The idea is easy to execute. Hold off on dessert. Make sure everyone is still comfortable at the table. Clear some but not all of the dirty dishes. Bring out the question basket and go around the table. If someone pulls out a question they don't want to answer, that's fine. Just have them grab another. Dad, you may want to start off to set the tone. Once the question is answered, other guests are welcome to ask followup questions or add their own thoughts.

If you're ambitious, make up your own questions. Or, the website TableTopics.com has several resources to consider for purchase. One option is to find a book of questions and put folded papers with page numbers in the basket. There are no hard-and-fast rules except that everyone participates and you may need to shush the table so each question-answerer gets full attention.

Families restore order

Dads should never stick their heads in the sand. We need to notice when our kids mess up. Sometimes we even need to initiate difficult conversations and demand corrective behavior. But a kid making a mistake shouldn't be cause for alarm. In most cases, the goal is to deal with it and not dwell on it.

You may be surprised to know that your kids do learn from their mistakes. By the time you get wind of it, they may have already taken steps to apologize, mitigate damages, and make the necessary changes so it doesn't happen again.

One of the great dad challenges of all time is to walk the tightrope of too much or too little vigilant parenting. You want to nip negative behavior early, rescuing them at the top of any slippery slope. On the other hand, you want to equip them to police themselves and make wise decisions on their own. After all, you're not always going to be there to stop them from taking a dare, walking into that tattoo parlor, posting an inappropriate photo, investing in swampland, or talking back to the traffic cop.

Here's a guiding principle that has served me well: A father needs to intervene if the aftermath is life-threatening, permanently damages your child's reputation, brings dishonor to God, or will cause them to miss a major opportunity in the near future. However, if their mess-up leads to some minor frustration with a coach, a failed grade on a homework assignment, or a friend with hurt feelings, then let them work it out for themselves. You can suggest they talk it out with the coach, teacher, or friend. But don't make any phone calls or rush to rescue your son or daughter. Especially if they don't ask for your help.

It's usually advantageous to let natural consequences take their course. It lets you off the hook. You don't have to be the bad guy coming up with just the right punishment. Once the lesson is learned, you could possibly step in and offer a word of encouragement or a helping hand. If they seem to have "gotten away with it," then you may need to add further consequences.

Need some real-life examples?

If an entire can of root beer gets knocked over in the family room, then the culprit may miss an afternoon with friends while they get a lesson in shampooing the carpet. However, if the guilty party tries to hide the stain or denies any involvement, then the penalty needs to expand far beyond the simple cleanup.

If your son gets kicked out of a game for arguing an umpire's call, then the league and his coach will probably execute just the right amount of disciplinary action. There's no need for you to pile on with any additional punishment. But also don't say, "That umpire was a complete idiot." (It's worth noting, you will run into some terrible referees and umpires. The lesson there is that we still need to respect authority.)

If your daughter says something thoughtless that hurts the feelings of her best friend, she's already feeling bad. You can't fix it. But she can. Let her know she has the power to make things right, and the sooner the better. Hurt feelings have a tendency to linger. A great perspective to share with your daughter might be, "Don't you think that your friendship is just as important to Kendra as it is to you? If you take the first step and apologize, she will probably be glad to forgive you." Say a little prayer that Kendra isn't too crushed to answer the door.

If your 20-year-old gets picked up for underage drinking, be glad that he called you. You want him to come to you for help. If he's basically a good kid and just got caught up making one bad decision, bail him out ASAP. If he's due for a good life lesson and it's a small-town police department with even-tempered cops and no hardened criminals, maybe let him sit there a couple hours. If it's his second offense, maybe he needs to stay the night. If it's a big-city lockup, hustle down and get him out of there before a bad situation gets even worse. In any case, if he's remorseful, don't treat him like a criminal. Treat him like a son.

After the dust settles and the appropriate consequences are underway, you can always revisit the experience. Not in the middle of the fiasco—but later say things like:

"Did you learn anything?"

"What would you do different next time?"

"Is there anything else you need to do or anyone else you need to apologize to in order to make this right?"

"Sometimes it helps to put yourself in the other person's shoes."

"How can I help?"

"You can count on me. Some day in the near future, I'm going to be counting on you."

"I love you. Nothing is going to change that."

The idea is to say these things with a smile and sense of partnership. Make it sound like the episode is now officially over and we're all eager to start fresh. Trust, optimism, and hope have been restored.

Families are forever

One of the best things about a family is that they will always be your family. Dad, I am 100 percent sure that—through thick and thin—you are going to make sure your kids know the light is always on and your door is always open. Right?

Can you imagine your little girl peeking in through a rainy window and you *not* inviting her in and making sure she's warm and well-fed? No way.

Can you imagine being the father of the prodigal son? Day after day, you pray for him to come home. Finally, you see him off in the distance—and you run into your big farmhouse *and lock the door*? Of course not.

Like the great parable told by Jesus in Luke chapter 15, you are not going to run away. You are going to do exactly what that father did.

> [The son] returned home to his father. And while he was still a long way off, his father saw him coming. Filled with love and compassion, he ran to his son, embraced him, and kissed him. His son said to him, "Father, I have sinned against both heaven and you, and I am no longer worthy of being called your son."
>
> But his father said to the servants, "Quick! Bring the finest robe in the house and put it on him. Get a ring for his finger and sandals for his feet. And kill the calf we have been fattening. We must celebrate with a feast, for this son of mine was dead and has now returned to life. He was lost, but now he is found." So the party began (Luke 15:20-24 NLT).

When your children come to you for help after they mess up, will you be in the mood to throw a party? That's the attitude of a father who will always be able to talk to his children. As a matter of fact, if you keep reading the next few paragraphs in the gospel of Luke, you'll discover the transcript of an honest, open conversation this father has with his envious older son. It's all good stuff. It's proof that Jesus intends families to work things out with patience, forgiveness, and the ability to quietly and respectfully talk things through.

We all know a family that has been split apart by ill feelings. Grown brothers and sisters who won't talk to each other. Adult children who haven't spoken to their parents for a decade. Why does that happen? Someone said something stupid. There was a misunderstanding. Someone was jealous or selfish or suffering from tunnel vision.

If that describes your family, then you may have some extra work to do. A wall hastily built years ago might be due to come down. Men, when it comes to conversations between the generations, maybe you need to come to terms with your relationship with your own father before you can expect complete and open dialogue with your son or daughter.

Some guys reading this might have wounds or scars that require healing. Opening your heart to a trusted friend, loving wife, wise pastor, or professional counselor might be the right thing to do. Some of you need to actually *talk* to your dad.

Every situation is different, and the last thing I want to do is oversimplify what you have experienced. But consider this: think for a moment about how much you love your children. You would give your life for them, right? Is it possible that your father—wherever he is and whatever he has done—had that same feeling for you? Or still does?

Which brings us full circle to your relationship with your own children. No matter what kind of experience you had with your own father while you were growing up, you have your own choices to make today.

Will you be the dad with the door that is always open? Maybe you could even take it a step further and be intentional about initiating conversations.

As dads, let's admit that we don't have all the answers. Yes, there are absolute truths, and sometimes a father will have to take a firm stand. But our conversations should rarely be dominated by statements that communicate "my way or the highway." However, what we do have to offer our children has enormous value. When it comes to the diverse issues explored in the coming chapters, we definitely have more experience than our kids. We've made some mistakes. We've learned a few things—and we're not afraid to learn a few more.

Keep reading and you'll uncover some ideas for dads to hang on to yourself. And some ideas for dads to share with your children. In the end, I pray your family will be stronger. And your relationship will be rooted in eternity.

The ten core chapters in this book conclude with a few questions offered for you to ask your children word for word. The talking points should help you anticipate how they might answer and how you might want to respond. The way these conversations play out are up to you. One-on-one. At the dinner table. During long car drives. Over milkshakes. Around a campfire. After midnight. Make sure to allow plenty of time. And include plenty of grace.

Questions to Get Them Talking

1. **What is a family?**

   Talking point: Wow, that's a toxic question these days. And you need to think through your answer before you ask it. But social scientists agree that the most effective family structure is a married mother and father committed to each other and working together to raise children under one roof. (Do I need to add that the father needs to be a human male and the mother a human female?) Is that controversial? I don't see how.

2. **What are some great things about our family? What are some frustrating things about our family?**

   Talking point: Hopefully, the first list is long. And the second is short. But you can see how both lists need to be brought out in the open. Depending on what's said, changes might need to be made. But not necessarily.

3. **Does our family have a reputation?**

   Talking point: Be ready, Dad. You might not like what you hear. It could be something encouraging or amusing like "Most kids think our house is a fun place to hang out" or "My teachers are always comparing me to Sara. Talk about pressure." Or maybe it's not so pleasant. Your kids might reveal that your family reputation is "They're a little rowdy," or "The kids are okay, but the dad is kind of a loudmouth,"

or maybe "Nice family. But they keep their Christmas deco-
rations up until March."

4. **Is there anything we can't talk about? Or shouldn't talk about?**

   Talking point: The amusing part about this question is that whatever they bring up, you're suddenly talking about! Still, honor their request. Daughters don't want to talk to you about their menstrual cycle, acne, or weight issues. Sons typically don't want to talk to their fathers about "feelings" or "why the coach isn't giving him more playing time." Asking your child if there's anything you should *not* be doing is a great gift. You're showing respect and giving them permission to be their own person.

5. **Are we fair with our discipline and punishments?**

   Talking point: Don't initiate this conversation in the middle of a tumultuous day. Have it when things are relatively calm. It's very likely, that you might hear, "I know I mess up. And I deserve to be punished. It's no fun. But it's fine." If your son or daughter responds with legitimate complaints about fairness, take note. But if they start talking about how their best friend is never punished for nasty behavior, you have been given an opportunity to talk about why you set such high standards and why God made parents in the first place. Plus, you know to be extra alert when your child hangs out with that undisciplined friend.

Conversations to Pursue

- *Talk about your family traditions.* What are the oldest traditions you can remember? Which ones are carried over from your parents? Or grandparents? Which ones are new? Maybe you've done something only a couple of times, but it sure feels like a tradition. Is that possible? Whose idea was it?

(Careful, giving credit to just one of your kids could start an argument.)

- *A family is like a puzzle!* All the pieces are designed to fit together. With some pieces, it takes a while to figure out where they fit in. The picture is not complete until every piece finds its place. Assembling the puzzle is part fun and part frustration. There are surprises along the way. When it comes together there is great satisfaction. Be careful about taking the metaphor too far. When the kids grow up, does it feel like breaking the puzzle up and putting it back in the box? What do you think?

- *In Ephesians 6:2, Paul points out that only one of the Ten Commandments comes with a promise.* The fifth commandment is "Honor your father and mother. Then you will live a long, full life in the land the LORD your God is giving you" (Exodus 20:12 NLT). Clearly, honoring the past generation makes life a whole lot easier for the next. Plus, if your kids honor you, they get real estate! (Right?)

- *Before your next car trip, get hold of a resource that has sharable questions.* I recommend *The Book of Questions* by Gregory Stock or *Chat Pack*, a set of thought-provoking cards by Bret Nicholaus and Paul Lowrie (the "Question Guys").

- *In Luke chapter 9 you can read the story of a guy who actually had the audacity to tell Jesus to wait.* Jesus is drafting disciples and one recruit says, "Yes, Lord, I will follow you, but first let me say goodbye to my family." Jesus' reply doesn't pull any punches. He says, "Anyone who puts a hand to the plow and then looks back is not fit for the Kingdom of God" (Luke 9:61-62 NLT). Does that sound a little mean? No. It's just honest. Once you decide to follow Jesus, keep your eyes on him. Put Christ ahead of everything—even your family.

On Competition

*"You are really never playing an opponent.
You are playing yourself."*

Arthur Ashe

*"I cheat my boys every chance I get.
I trade with the boys and skin 'em and
I just beat 'em every time I can.
I want to make 'em sharp."*

John D. Rockefeller

The playground at Lincoln school has no grass. It's all asphalt, but that's never been a problem. Because for decades, the third, fourth, and fifth graders played kickball (a.k.a. kick-soccer-baseball.) The rules are similar to baseball, except the pitcher rolls one of those red kickballs to the batter, who boots it into the field. The kicker runs to first and advances at their own risk. If the ball is caught on the fly, the batter is out. Or a fielder can throw the ball at a runner if they are not on a base. You've probably played some version of this timeless game.

Three of my kids—Max, Isaac, and Rae Anne—honed their kicking, ball-catching, and other useful skills on that patch of asphalt with the yellow painted lines. But as it turns out, no child will ever play kickball at Lincoln school again. It's been banned. They painted over the diamond. At last report, the school administration no longer allows balls of any kind on the blacktop during recess.

Apparently the students were getting too competitive. My understanding is that the underpaid recess monitors didn't like the aggressive nature of kickball and the administration had other more pressing issues. So without too much debate, students are now limited to two options at recess. Wimpy organized athletic activities supervised directly by recess monitors. Or huddling in small groups to gossip.

This turn of events seems to be saying that it's no longer worthwhile for older elementary school students to learn how to play fair, keep score, and work out any differences with their peers. From my limited vantage point, it's just another example of authority figures refusing to acknowledge the value of competition. That's the same attitude that brought us the unfortunate tradition of handing out "participation trophies." Oh. My. Gosh. If you're in the trophy-making business, I apologize. But somewhere around 1980 (or maybe earlier) a well-intentioned coach got the idea that every kid deserves a piece of glistening hardware just for showing up. Which means there is no longer any expectation to extend any effort whatsoever.

In my experience, competition is not something to be banned, shunned, or avoided. But unfortunately that's the trend. So I encourage you to ask your kids. In the course of a school week, do they have legitimate opportunities to compete? That could include a spontaneous game of tag on the playground, a game of speed chess at lunch, or even a game of "tabletop football" played with a piece of notebook paper folded into a triangle. Back in my day, part of the classroom experience was spelling bees, geography bees, dictionary races, book-reading contests, and memorization competition. Teachers even dared post the best artwork and cleverest science project in the classroom showcase. Today, I fear that school administrators are afraid of suggesting that children have different levels of talent, skills, gifts, perseverance, and experience. The result? Instead of encouraging excellence, they're applauding mediocrity.

Even physical education teachers currently spend their limited time instructing students on nutrition, stretching, and cardio exercises. Those are admirable goals, of course. But I'm not sure how much of it sinks in with a bunch of middle schoolers. I do know that the ages of eight through twelve are critical when it comes to developing self-confidence and choosing what dreams a kid might pursue in high school and beyond. Which leads to the question, How can a boy or girl identify their gifts and talents if they don't measure themselves against their peers?

Most of the dads I know want our kids to be active participants in life and not just watch the world pass them by without digging deep and investing in a worthy cause. Competition doesn't just teach boys and girls how to compete. It teaches them who they are and who they might become. And more.

The bond of competition

On November 17, 2013, a half-mile wide tornado destroyed more than 1000 homes in Washington, Illinois, including the homes of more than ten players on the roster of the local high school football team. Six days later, the Washington Panthers were scheduled to play in the state semifinals for the first time since 1985. Some folks in town objected to the frivolity of playing a football game when so much suffering had occurred and so much work was to be done. But to those who understand the power of healthy competition, a good football game was exactly the right therapy for a hurting community. So the undefeated Panthers prepared to do battle with the undefeated team from Springfield, ironically called the "Cyclones."

On the field, both teams played tough. But off the field, the competition opened the door to compassion. Knowing that many of the Panther fans had lost their homes and cars less than a week earlier, the Cyclones supplied seven buses so family and friends who would cheer for the other team could make the 90-minute trip to the game. The Springfield boosters also arranged for pregame and postgame meals, not just for the visiting athletes, but for all 2,000 Washington fans. The Springfield team displayed a banner reading "We Care" and held several fundraising initiatives, raising thousands of dollars for their longtime rivals. The Cyclones' coach called for both teams to huddle for prayer midfield after the game and said, "This is a great life lesson. I want our players to be better men than football players."

That lesson doesn't happen without competition. Fierce rivals respecting, honoring, and genuinely caring for each other is an age-old tradition in sports. Here are two more examples worth sharing with your kids.

In 2008, Western Oregon University softball player Sara Tucholsky hit the first home run of her career, which seemingly would drive in three runs and likely eliminate Central Washington University from making the playoffs. As she rounded first, Tucholsky collapsed with a possible torn knee ligament, leaving her home run in jeopardy. The umpire said she would be called out if any teammates came onto the field to assist her. The ump indicated a pinch runner could take her place, but the at-bat would then count only as a single.

That's when the first baseman from Central Washington, Mallory Holtman, asked the umpire if she and a teammate could assist their injured rival. Holtman and shortstop Liz Wallace literally picked up Tucholsky and carried her around the base paths, stopping to let her touch each base with her uninjured leg. "In the end, it is not about winning and losing so much," Holtman said. "It was about this girl. She hit it over the fence and was in pain, and she deserved a home run." The incident was publicized widely and earned an ESPY Award for 2008 Best Moment in Sports.

In Pennsylvania, 220-pounder Joey Kaufman anticipated wrestling Gus Bostdorf for the 2013 state championship. Rankings at the beginning of the season predicted the two adversaries would lock horns in a marquee matchup. Instead, Bostdorf, undergoing chemotherapy for a tumor pressing on his left lung, watched the state finals from the stands. After the awards ceremony, Kaufman climbed into the stands to find his longtime rival and gave him the medal. Kaufman explained, "It killed me a little bit when I found out he had a tumor. He made me a better wrestler with the fight he gave me. I pray for him to get better. It's hard to see him, his family and friends go through this."

Despite these examples, it's possible to see competition as a force that causes division and disharmony. But it's more likely that those conditions already existed. When poor winners or sore losers compete, their true colors emerge.

In this digital age, we see plenty of evidence of behavior on both ends of the spectrum. Hotheaded fathers cursing out referees and throwing punches in the stands. But we also see rival teams working together to allow a special-needs student to experience the joy of scoring a touchdown or crossing the plate.

Dad, with just a little effort you can find video clips of both of those extremes and share them with your own young athlete. Emotionally charged YouTube videos are a great springboard for conversation. While you're at it, give your son or daughter permission to let you know if you ever embarrass them in the bleachers. Also, make them promise to tell you if they are ever part of a positive, uplifting example of great sportsmanship. Those moments happen more often than you might think.

Competition develops

...respect for a hardworking opponent.
...an appreciation for discipline and goal-setting.
...a realization that we all have different gifts.
...teammates who are friends for life.

Winning is fun

It never fails. On the first day of practice for far too many organized youth sports teams, the well-meaning coach stands in front of his eager athletes and parents and says, "The most important thing is to have fun."

And I just want to gag.

Hold on, hear me out. Give me a couple paragraphs to convince you that any coach who says, "The most important thing is to have fun," is wrong for two reasons.

First, those words suggest that winning is not important. Let me remind you that winning is the goal. That's why we keep score. Dads, we want our kids to be winners. And not just in preschool soccer. We want our kids to be winners in life. We want them to achieve positive outcomes in school, careers, and raising our grandchildren. We want our kids to do more than just show up. We want them to set goals, practice, strategize, identify their strengths and weaknesses, overcome setbacks, partner with teammates, and appreciate the satisfaction of doing their best. In other words, we want them to learn to compete.

The second problem with a coach's saying, "The most important thing is to have fun," is that he's obviously overlooking one of the great rewards of winning. Hey, Coach—"It's more fun to win than lose!"

Winning is important

Which brings me to the strategic chalk talk I developed that I believe every young athlete should hear during their introduction to organized sports. I used this talk often with wrestling, baseball, and girls' softball. It definitely works better with boys, maybe because it's easier to get them jazzed up about sports.

During the first or second practice, after gaining their trust, I would gather the team and quietly pose this question, "What do you think? Is winning important? Is it important to win?" The boys would look around, slightly unsure of how to respond. Invariably, a couple of them would say, "No." Then a couple more. And within seconds most of the team would come to an agreement: "Winning isn't important."

I loved that moment. Clearly those boys had been watching too much Barney the purple dinosaur or had been exposed to too much wimpy talk about playing fair and not being too aggressive from some saccharine preschool teacher. As one of their first coaches, I took it upon myself to correct their inaccurate perception.

My little speech would go something like this: "Gentlemen, let me tell you about winning. Winning is important. Winning is a good thing. Scoring more points than your opponent and earning a victory is the goal. That's why we practice, learn the rules, work hard, and sweat. Your goal is to improve. To sharpen your skills. To get strong so that you can win your next competition. Gentlemen, let me assure you it is fun to win. *I* like to win. Do *you* like to win? Does your mom or dad want you to win? When you get out there and face your opponent, is it your goal to lose or to win?"

Now by this time, the boys are eager and excited. The troops have been rallied. They're responding with yeses and cheers. Then with a rising tone that would make Knute Rockne proud, I ask the initial question one more time, "So! Is winning important?" With fervor, some of them even jump to their feet and shout, "YES!"

That's when I stop. And in a much calmer voice I would say, "I agree. Winning is important. But I'm wondering if there are some things that are even more important than winning." That's when the light would go on. Those sharper-than-you-might-think elementary-school boys would propose mature concepts like "doing your best…working hard…being a good sport…family…friends…teamwork…shaking hands." And I would respond, "Yes, yes, yes, and yes! Winning is important, but there are things that are even more important."

Over the years, some of those young athletes responded with other surprising answers. A few said, "God is more important than wrestling." With delight, I added my affirmation. One boy said, "Music." After a pause, I said, "Yes. Music and art and other beautiful things are probably more important than winning a baseball game or wrestling match." One eloquent young man said, "Trying hard and then losing and trying hard again is more important than winning." That's good stuff.

I remember well that parents often stuck around for those first few practices. Never did any mom or dad try to stop me in the middle of my strategic chalk talk on winning. Thank goodness. But many of them would come up after that session or at the end of the season to express their thanks. Being a coach who has the right priorities is an unforgettably rewarding experience.

Some of those boys and girls went on to earn medals, trophies, and college scholarships. Others simply burned off some energy over the summer or during a winter's worth of Saturday mornings. All of them, I hope, got a dose of what it means to set priorities and meet a challenge head-on. That's a principle that applies in any endeavor they ever choose to tackle.

Thinking back, it took me several years to develop this approach that blends teaching sportsmanship with a winning attitude. I offer it to you, no charge. If you ever find yourself coaching a group of kids under ten, it could make all the difference in whether your season is a success or not. (And I'm not talking about wins and losses.) It's not nearly as effective with a team of children older than ten. By then, most kids have already decided whether they are going to be a competitor or live on the sidelines of life.

The group dynamic helps bring the lesson home. But the principle also works one-on-one with your own son or daughter. You can start by simply asking, "Is winning important?" and seeing how they respond.

Dad as sparring partner

Preparing for an upcoming bout, a boxer will spend hours in the practice ring with his or her sparring partner. Their goal is not to do physical harm to each other; instead it's to hone their skills, get into the best physical shape possible, and discover their own best strategies for victory. Boxers work on their jab, uppercut, and roundhouse. They check footwork and blocking. They determine whether or not they can deliver a knockout punch. In other words, practice makes perfect. Because you care so much about your child, you are the ideal foil to help them determine their strengths and weaknesses while competing in a safe environment.

Continuing with the metaphor. Sparring partners sometimes go half or three-quarter speed to allow their colleague to work on strategic moves. Both boxers are well protected with headgear and extra padding. Both boxers grow in the process without risk. Just so, a father can challenge his daughter or son in any physical or intellectual competition, and both of you will gain wisdom and experience in the battle.

In early competitions, Dad should expect to emerge victorious. Whether it's checkers, driveway basketball, Ping-Pong, laser tag, trivia games, Monopoly, or Scrabble, go ahead and dominate. It's to your child's advantage if you catch more fish, hit a straighter drive, or stack a higher house of cards. Don't get carried away, but go ahead and out-perform them while you still can. It will give the young competitor something to shoot for and a reason to keep asking you to play. Just don't forget to celebrate when they pass you by. Because in the end, you want them to do exactly that. Right?

By the way, there are two cases in which you may not hold a distinct advantage. One is video games. Young minds and reflexes often outduel dads. They also have friends who reveal shortcuts and secrets you may never know. When you accept the challenge to pick up a game controller, you should pretty much expect to lose. Just make sure you're a good sport, okay?

The other contest which has a more level playing field is rock/paper/scissors. The random act of throwing a clenched fist, a flat palm, or a sideways peace sign gives any child a chance to beat their father fair and square. If you teach a four-year-old, it will soon be a favorite pastime. So be prepared to play anytime and anywhere. (It's actually a nice distraction when you're in line at an amusement park.)

But the most important truth about rock/paper/scissors is a secret you must never share with your child. Here it is. When a new game begins, every kid between age four and nine will start by throwing "scissors" 93 percent of the time. Guaranteed. If you feel like flexing your superiority, go ahead and throw "rock." If you want to give them the momentary thrill of victory, throw "paper." (If I'm wrong, track me down and I will refund the price of this book. If I'm right, buy another copy to give to a friend.)

Men, as your child's first and best sparring partner, be the kind of competitor you want them to be. Tenacious. Spirited. Honest. Humble. Courageous. Willing to practice. Eager to learn.

The rules of competition

One of the other great lessons of healthy competition is spelled out clearly in 2 Timothy 2:5, "Anyone who competes as an athlete does not receive the victor's crown except by competing according to the rules."

There may come a day when your daughter hits the pole vault height that should have won the track meet but is disqualified for wearing an illegal piece of jewelry—a multicolored string friendship bracelet. (True story.) Or your son's free throw doesn't count because he stepped on the line. (Happens every day.) Or perhaps more painful, your college-bound shortstop is thrown out of a game for yelling at an umpire or is kicked off the team for committing an athletic code violation.

When these things happen, Dad, I encourage you not to storm onto the field, chase down the official in the parking lot, or hire a lawyer to get your child reinstated. (I've seen all those things.) Instead, let the lesson and consequences speak for themselves. There are much more important things at stake than one game or one season.

Competition is the absolute best place to learn that rules exist. Rules that are written and unwritten. Rules that seem unfair. And, yes, even rules set down by a loving God who knows everything about your children and wants only the best for them. As your child competes, look for teachable moments. They're everywhere.

Competition in the classroom

Just to confirm, competition is not limited to athletics. There are plenty of other occasions when you need to anticipate a competitive environment and equip your child to hold their own. Early in your child's school career, you want to set them up for success.

Here's the plan which you can use throughout their elementary and middle-school years. Most curriculums have students learning "opposites" in kindergarten, "multiplication" late in second grade, "centripetal force" in fourth grade, and "how to bisect an angle with a compass and a straight edge" sometime in middle school. Your school district should be able to tell you exactly what they teach and when.

When a teacher introduces new concepts to a class full of kids, some kids pick up on it faster than others. Educational professionals won't describe it as a competition, but don't kid yourself. It totally is. Dad, wouldn't you prefer your own kid to be in the winner's bracket when it comes to new topics that are introduced in the classroom?

Here's an idea. Not the week before. Not the semester before. But YEARS before, go ahead and teach a few of these concepts to your kids. Make it a game!

Do you know a three-year-old? Ask them, "What's the opposite of *up*?" They won't know. Tell them with great sincerity, "The opposite of up is *down*!" Then ask them, "What is the opposite of *cold*?" They won't know. Tell them the "The opposite of cold is *hot*!" Do the same with big/little, loud/quiet, slow/fast, closed/open, nice/mean, clean/dirty, yes/no, off/on, and so on. Use your best vocal expressiveness, use your hands, look in their face, mime the answer as you say it.

After four or five examples, suddenly their little face lights up and they understand! It's amazing. It's a rush for them and for you. In a couple years, when the kindergarten teacher starts teaching "opposites," your kid is going to be top of the class. Suddenly, they will be earmarked as a bright student worthy of special attention the rest of their school career. This is more than just a conversation to have with your kids, it's strategic fathering. You're not giving your child fake praise. They have achieved excellence, and you made it happen!

Do the same with multiplication when your kid is in first grade. But don't ask, "What is five times two?" That sounds confusing. Instead, ask "What is five, two times?" Use your hands as demonstration. Then ask, "What is four, two times?" Then ask, "What is four, three times!" A sharp first-grader (your kid) will get it. Be warned, though—you've turned learning into a game and they may never want to stop. That's when you know you have put them way ahead of the curve.

One more example. On the next nice day, invite your second-grader out to your driveway to wash your car. Ask them if they think you can hold the bucket of water upside down over your head without spilling it. They will laugh and say "No way, Daddy!" Then spin that bucket over your head without losing a drop. They'll be amazed, and you will have demonstrated centrifugal and centripetal force. (Look it up, if you don't remember.)

Healthy competition

...brings your family together.
...leads to many teachable moments.
...helps kids learn to handle disappointment.
...builds authentically earned self-esteem.

Not everything is a competition

There are opportunities for teachable moments and healthy competition all day every day. But Dad, make sure to leave room for a little fun. Your child's snowman doesn't have to be the biggest. They can throw a vase on a potter's wheel just for the satisfaction of trying something new. They can skip, roll, and slide down a sand dune simply for the joy and exhilaration of it.

And not everything has to be a teachable moment either. If you choose, you can explain how rolling and elevating that third snowball for the snowman's head requires some planning, estimation, physics, and brute force. You can get all serious about proper pottery-making techniques and describe it as a skill that can take years to master. While climbing that sand dune you can have a scientific conversation about beach erosion, gravity, and inertia. But the better choice might be to just do it. The carrot nose might be crooked, the clay pot may leak, and your kids might get sand down their swimsuits. It's all good.

Competing for life

Ask any successful middle school youth pastor. About half the time spent with young people consists of silly contests, team-building games, sports tournaments, and seeing who can sing louder or eat faster. They know that particular age group is wired to engage in competition. The international youth ministry, AWANA, brilliantly taps into the desire for kids to compete in games, races, scripture memory, and other projects. Boy Scouts, Trail Life USA, Girl Scouts, and American Heritage

Girls are all about collecting badges and moving up the ranks. Competing with others and with yourself.

Maybe it comes down to this. Life isn't for wimps. There's good and evil. There's right and wrong. Competition makes individuals stronger to stand up for what they believe with courage and conviction.

> Be strong in the Lord and in his mighty power. Put on the full armor of God, so that you can take your stand against the devil's schemes. For our struggle is not against flesh and blood, but against the rulers, against the authorities, against the powers of this dark world and against the spiritual forces of evil in the heavenly realms (Ephesians 6:10-12).

When your children face the spiritual forces of evil—and they will—do you want them to be well-prepared and ready for battle? While they're still under your roof, Dad, train them to put on the full armor of God and take a stand. Cheer them on and claim victory for Christ.

Questions to Get Them Talking

1. **Would you rather play a game for fun or play to win?**
   Talking point: Against your dear son or daughter, promise that you will always play to win. But admit that someday when battling against your grandchild, you might allow them to win by the slimmest of margins just to see the joy on their face of beating Grandpa.

2. **Is it okay to beat your best friend in a game or sporting activity? Even if it makes them feel bad?**
   Talking point: Worse than making them feel bad when they lose is making them feel even worse when they find out that you let them win.

3. **Would you rather win by a small margin or crush your competition? Is your answer different depending on the competition and the competitor?**

Talking point: If your competition is a classy, worthy opponent, there may be a small bit of empathy when you defeat them. So maybe you shouldn't pile on additional points. Dad, this may be a time you confess that because of a long-standing rivalry, you took great joy (probably too much joy) in defeating an opponent by an outrageous margin.

4. **Is it ever okay to quit in the middle of a match?**

   Talking point: When chess masters play, few matches are played until a "checkmate." Often a match is designated a "draw" by agreement of the competitors. Sometimes to the surprise of the audience, a player who senses defeat will reach out and lay his king down on the chessboard, thus ending the match. But most of the time, we should play hard until the final whistle.

5. **During a competition is it ever appropriate to say, "I didn't do my best, but that's okay"?**

   Talking point: It's impossible to give 100 percent to every endeavor 100 percent of the time. Sometimes we have to choose when to stop pushing for excellence and simply say, "It's okay if I don't get first place." On the other hand, when you commit to a competition, it really is important to give it everything you've got—in the moment, to the best of your ability. You owe it to yourself, your teammates, your future, and your competitor.

Conversations to Pursue

- *Think back to when you were the age of your children.* What were your favorite games, sports, contests, and opportunities to compete? Any magnificent victories? Any devastating losses? Did you handle those situations well?

- *How are your children different from each other?* How are they different from their friends? In a group of friends, some will be smarter, some more athletic, some more well-rounded. That's okay, right?

- *Tell your children the story of the football players and boosters who came together* after the tornado damaged more than 100 homes in Washington, Illinois. Or the softball players and wrestlers who showed good sportsmanship. You should be able to search online for these stories—or find similar stories in your local paper. Share true stories of selfless competitors and see where it goes!

- *First Corinthians 9:24 tells us,* "Do you not know that in a race all the runners run, but only one gets the prize? Run in such a way as to get the prize." What prize is this letter from Paul talking about? (Read the next few verses together.) And how can healthy competition prepare us to do God's work?

- *When you sense your child is not giving their best effort, see if you can find out why.* Tread lightly though, Dad. Don't accuse them of being lazy or not caring. There are many possible reasons. Maybe they don't know the rules and are afraid of making a mistake. Maybe they just didn't know where to start. Or their schedule was just too jammed. Are there other—totally different—things they would rather be doing? Are they giving up after multiple attempts that left them frustrated and feeling inadequate?

Conversation 3

On Creativity

*"Everybody is creative, and everybody is talented.
I just don't think everybody is disciplined."*

Al Hirschfeld

*"Creativity is allowing yourself to make mistakes.
Art is knowing which ones to keep."*

Scott Adams

When your four-year-old proudly presents you with a drawing of what looks like a porcupine playing piano and eating pizza on the porch, you have two choices: 1) Crush their little creative spirit. 2) Launch them into a world of stimulating curiosity, expanding possibilities, and thinking slightly or significantly outside the box.

Going out on a limb, I'm going to make this decision for you. Dad, choose #2. Here's how that conversation should play out.

Your first fatherly response to their fantastical drawing is actually quite obvious. You *oooh* and *aaah*. But after that, you need to be a little more calculated with your response. Your next goal is to find out what is actually in the drawing without letting them know you don't know. So don't say, "What is it?" Instead invite the little artist up on your lap and say, "Whoa. This is most excellent. Tell me about it." Then start picking up on their verbal cues. Let them point to the indecipherable kayak, Ferris wheel, marching band, or wildebeest. Ask them open-ended questions that get them thinking and explaining. "How did you choose these two colors?" "These lines are straight and these are curvy. Why did you choose that?"

The idea is to partner with them in the discovery of their own creative abilities and help them see how they have control over the creative choices they make. You can point out elements of their artwork that are bold and decisive, even suggesting that their efforts have led you to think new thoughts. Let them know that—like all great works of art—their masterpiece has given you a new perspective on life, the world, or some other grand concept.

After the creative brainstorming session, there's one more critical element of this conversation. You need to bring it to a satisfying closure. The best way to attach value to any artistic endeavor is to attach value to the art itself.

In the case of the budding Picasso sitting on your lap, that's easy. The artist is going to say, "You can keep it, Daddy." You accept the gift graciously, continue to ponder it while they skip off to their next project, and then slide the artwork into that file folder you have with their name on it. Don't have one? Make one. A color-coded file folder for each of your children is the perfect receptacle for handmade cards, love notes, team rosters, recital programs, newspaper clippings, ticket stubs, scorecards, and all the stuff that often ends up cluttering the kitchen counter.

When it comes to your child's early creative efforts, file folders are a boon to fathers everywhere. You don't want to toss it. You don't want it taped to the wall in your man cave. One option would be to convince the young artist that it would be "a perfect gift for Mom!" In a rare instance you'll want to have an exceptional piece of art professionally mounted and framed. The result is a forever keepsake, which is a worthy investment. But for most two-dimensional projects, the file folder is your best answer.

As described, the entire process of encouraging creativity in a preschooler is simple and painless. In five minutes, you've successfully nudged them toward a new understanding and appreciation for the creative process.

Creativity is

...making choices that lead to something new.
...inspiring an audience to think new ideas.
...not accidental.
...a talent you can use today.
...a talent that gets sharpened the more you use it.

As they get older and their creativity takes on new and varied forms, the principles remain. But empowering your children may take a little more time and a dose of humility on your part. You may be clever enough to fake your way through a conversation with a preschooler about their crayon art. But unless you're an established painter, writer, sculptor, musician, performer, or gallery owner, you won't be able to fake your way through a critique of your teenager's artistic endeavor.

When your ballerina asks how you like her pirouette or fouetté, it's really okay to say, "Sweetie, I like what I saw. But I'm not quite sure what those words mean."

When the eager poet living under your roof asks your opinion on his latest sonnet, take your time, read it thoughtfully, and then ask open-ended questions about theme, subtext, and intended audience. Just don't ask why it has only 14 lines. (All sonnets have 14 lines.)

When that young-adult photographer you raised invites you to a gallery opening, don't embarrass them by being loudly shocked by the nude photos. Later, you can certainly let them know you were a little surprised. By the way: they knew you would be.

If your children are courageous enough to ask your opinion, congratulations. You have built a relationship of trust and respect. They trust you not to trash or belittle their efforts. They expect you to add value to their project, not devalue what they're trying to achieve.

You do want them to come to you, right? If not, skip to the next chapter.

Hit and miss

Speaking from experience, I have chosen to make myself available to any of my kids at any time to consider any of their creative endeavors and offer my brilliant and not-so-brilliant feedback. From Lego towers to sculptures made of wood, nails, and string. From poignant short stories to garish bedroom paint jobs. Sometimes they would request my opinion while a project was still in the planning stages. Sometimes they had no desire for my response until after their one and only public unveiling or performance.

All five of my children had different levels of confidence in their own abilities in a variety of media and art forms. They each had their strengths, but they also weren't afraid to try new things. They also knew sometimes their dad knew what he was talking about and sometimes he was just making it up.

Let me share two specific occasions in which my eldest son, Alec, presented me with one of his many creative works and asked my opinion. Both times I was honored. One time I responded effectively; the other time not so much.

The first was the debut CD of his working rock band, Fool's Crow. Alec and three other students at the University of Illinois had already established themselves as one of Champaign-Urbana's more popular bands. I listened to each cut several times with a mixture of awe, jealousy, curiosity, skepticism, and pride. My son had created something that was far beyond my ability and imagination. The album was quite good.

But as his father, there were many factors to consider. Being a rock star was not part of my plan for Alec. (No surprise there.) I wondered how this might impact his studies. His life. Clearly these four young men were not just goofing around. They were putting significant effort into improving their craft and establishing a following. They were getting paid to play. The lyrics were not trashy, but they weren't specifically

God-honoring either. Alec invited Rita and me down to watch a show and it happened to be on our anniversary. Fool's Crow played mostly original compositions, but that night from the stage, Alec dedicated a song to us. One of my favorites, an old Elton John tune called "Your Song." My bride and I danced in the aisle and were moved to tears.

So how did I critique their album? I found a dozen things I liked about it. I made note of a couple creative choices that I wasn't sure about. I let him know that I was awed by the follow-through and professionalism he and his band mates were demonstrating. And then I heard words coming out of my mouth that you may want to remember and use if you ever find yourself in a similar situation. I said, "I look forward to seeing how God uses this creative gift he has given you."

The critique turned into a conversation. As we talked, I learned about his motivations and dreams. He opened himself up to a few more of my thoughts and opinions. The result was that Alec always kept us informed of his show dates and allowed us into his inner circle of friends and fans. The band moved to Chicago, added a couple new members, changed their name a couple times, and played a variety of packed venues. I still have many of their original songs running through my mind. I cherish the evenings spent watching Alec and his band mates perform.

Then there was another time Alec invited me to review one of his artistic endeavors, a Broadway-style musical he had written. He delivered to me a full-length two-act bound manuscript complete with cast list, stage direction, dialogue, soliloquies, and lyrics. The considerable time he had put into both the content and presentation was evident. I picked it up again recently and was reminded of how I felt when I first read it a decade ago. As with the rock album, I experienced appreciation, wonder, and pride in his significant accomplishment. Reading it again, I have an even greater appreciation for the subtext and themes my son explored in his script.

And I also remember the three-hour creative lunch meeting we had at the old Denny's on Route 38 in Lombard. We met halfway between Chicago and St. Charles and I enthusiastically unloaded an overwhelming amount of notes and ideas on how to take his master-piece and make it even better. I scratched dozens of notes in the margin. I added characters and plot twists. I suggested new scenes. I wondered about the motivations of his hero. I questioned whether the last scene—the focal point of the entire production—left the audience unsatisfied. And I told him I was looking forward to reading the next draft. Which, of course, never got written.

Now, I am taking no credit for the success of Alec's band and accepting no blame for a potential Broadway smash closing before it even opened. There are far too many other factors to consider. Creativity doesn't begin or end with one opinion or conversation. But I do believe there are snippets of conversations that can lead a young artist to dig deep within themselves, rededicate themselves to creative excellence, and take their work to the next level. I also believe words—especially from a father—can knock a promising project right off its tracks. Consider the power in these phrases:

"There's something really nice happening here."

"Wow. Son, this is special."

"It's good. Very good. I wish I had that kind of creativity."

"I don't know what your next steps are. But this needs to be seen/heard/read/tasted by someone who can help you take it to the next level. If I can help in any way, let me know."

Or conversely:

"I don't get it."

"What did the other kids do? Is this what the teacher wanted?"

"It seems to me like you're spending a lot of time on this that could be used more productively."

"Shouldn't you be writing from experience? You've never been to Idaho."

"Is this what you went to college for?"

A great parenting principle I keep coming back to is this. In every interaction with your kids, you have a choice to pull them toward you or push them away. Dad, when critiquing your child's artistic endeavors, choose your words carefully.

Wasting talent

Judging thoughtlessly or harshly is one way to douse your son or daughter's creative fire. The other is by stoking another kind of destructive fire. The fear of failure.

I was briefly scorched by that fear back in fifth grade. To their credit, my mom and dad recognized a flicker of artistic talent in yours truly. And initially, they came through with flying colors (pun intended) that Christmas. I was thrilled to unwrap the Jon Gnagy Master Art Studio. It came in a fake wood-grain cardboard carrying case with a metal clasp and black plastic handle. Inside were rows of real oil paints, watercolors, pastel chalks, and sketching pencils. Instruction books, sketchpads, assorted brushes, mixing trays, erasers, and sharpeners completed the set. It was awesome. I remember it well because I studied it for hours on end. I looked at it. I imagined all I would create with it. But I never actually used it. I was afraid to.

On that Christmas, more than four decades ago, my dad cheerfully and with the best intentions said four words that unintentionally snuffed out any creative spark. He said, "Now don't waste it." With that admonition echoing in the back of my head, I dutifully committed to protecting and preserving those precious paints and brushes until I could use them properly.

Dad could have said, "Have fun. Experiment. Go crazy. When you run out, we'll get more." Those words would have inspired me to take risks, explore my gifts, and if some technique didn't work, simply start again. Today, my work could be hanging in museums around the world or I could be a starving artist in Key West. But instead, the paints and pastels in the Jon Gnagy Master Art Studio went untested. Same goes for my potential as a visual artist.

Let me be clear, there's no remorse. God had other plans for me and they have worked out quite nicely, thank you. My father, having been raised in the Great Depression, was quite accurate with his words. Resources shouldn't be wasted. But what Dad didn't realize is that our most valuable resources are not stuff—paints, paper, clay, wood, film, or canvas. Our greatest resources are the personal gifts and talents God has given each one of us.

One of our most important jobs as a father is to help our kids unleash their natural gifts and talents, not hold them captive. Our children should never fear the creative process. But fear, regret, and embarrassment may sometimes be exactly what we're conveying, isn't it? Even when we're trying to be helpful.

"Don't waste those oil paints!"

"It looks like fun. But is that something you can make a living at?"

"That girl is your age, right? Wow. If you practice more, you could be that good."

"That's fine for your sister. But come on, son. Be realistic."

"That's fine for now. You need to get that arty stuff out of your system."

Fathers who guide their children away from the arts intentionally or otherwise are doing them a great disservice. Even if you see scant evidence of creative ability, please nurture and encourage their colorful dabbles and piano plinking. You certainly shouldn't expect your child's first painting, video short, house design, poem, or short story to be a masterpiece. First efforts are never a waste. Second efforts take courage, which should always be applauded. And third efforts often lead to a fulfilling adventure that may last a lifetime.

The truth is that a child involved in the arts not only learns how to be more creative, they also are more likely to attend college, get into med school, stay off drugs, tobacco, and alcohol, and behave in the classroom.[1] That's especially true for music, which the ancient Greek scholar Pythagoras saw as a link to advanced math and architectural skills.

And what's so bad about a career in the arts anyway? Sure, no dad wants their child to become a starving artist living in an abandoned warehouse. But is that really what would happen? Sure, chances are slim that they'll become rich and famous for their art. However, your hardworking son or daughter could very likely make a decent living as a writer, ballerina, or architect. What's more, because of your undying support, they might even dedicate a book to you, invite you to the opening of their new dance studio, or give you a personal guided tour of the office park they designed.

No matter what vocation they choose, the ability to imagine and innovate will serve them well. From accountant to football coach. From homemaker to ophthalmologist. The ability to look at a problem from a variety of angles is a direct result of developing one's creative brainpower early in life. When a roadblock appears on the job, at home, or wherever, someone with a creative background—like your son or daughter—has a better chance of coming up with a fresh idea that turns that roadblock into a bridge of opportunity.

Real-life creativity

Back in the 1990s, Colorado Casual came out with a line of subtle witness wear called "Tucked-Out Tees." The T-shirts featured amusing quotes printed boldly across the chest of the wearer and designed to initiate a conversation, but they also included a related Scripture verse printed on a patch near the bottom hem of each shirt.

Probably my favorite was "Living for three-day weekends" followed below by "Christ died for our sins, just as the Scriptures said. He was buried, and he was raised from the dead on the third day.—1 Corinthians 15:3-4 NLT." Another favorite was "I can be bought," which is explained by the verse, "He is so rich in kindness and grace that he purchased our freedom with the blood of his Son and forgave our sins.—Ephesians 1:7 NLT."

The trademarked motto for the line of 18 T-shirts was "Tuck it out and share the word." If you happened to own one, you'll be amused to hear that "Tucked-Out Tees" was my idea and we sold somewhere around 8000 shirts in all. One of the most gratifying moments of the endeavor was when I invited my teenage son Alec to come up with some ideas. The navy-blue shirt with the orange words "Umm…Aardvark" became one of the bestsellers. The patch said, "So the LORD God formed from the soil every kind of animal and bird. He brought them to Adam to see what he would call them, and Adam chose a name for each one.—Genesis 2:19 NLT."*

The Payleitner T-shirt idea-generating didn't stop there. One lazy

---

* NLT 1st edition, 1996.

Sunday afternoon, I happened to see a small newspaper ad requesting T-shirt slogans for the What on Earth catalog. I responded with a page of ideas just off the top of my head. They actually paid me a small stipend for slogans like "I don't tan, I rust," "Yes, I know I need a haircut," "Honorary Oompa Loompa," and "Only Three Bad Habits."

Once again, I invited participation from my kids. Over a five-year period, they generated hundreds of ideas, and What on Earth selected and produced quite a few. From Alec came "Peaked in High School," "Piano Lesson Dropout," and "When do telemarketers eat dinner?" Randall contributed, "Did you find that short pier yet?" "I can't complain. But still do," and the very popular "I make up my own dance moves." Max came up with "Have You Seen My Marbles?" "I owned a pet rock," and "Great story. Please tell it again." Isaac added, "Honestly, I find you disturbing," "Sleeps with a nightlight," and "This shirt passed the sniff test."

If it sounds like I'm bragging about the creativity of my offspring, I guess I am a little. But the principle is universal. What are you doing—on the job, in your hobby, in your home—that needs a creative spark and a fresh perspective? Even though you've been their primary mentor and teacher, those children living in your house and eating around your dinner table have all kinds of clever ideas that would never cross your mind.

Try this exercise. Write down three challenges at work. Things involving communication, technology, transportation, organization, leadership, training, media, personal interaction, whatever. This week at dinner, express one of those problems in the simplest terms to your family. Then ask for ideas. Use creative brainstorming principles such as "no judging," "piggyback on each other's ideas," and "wacky ideas are welcome." You may be—no, you *will* be—surprised by what your kids come up with. Plus, you're all talking! And that's a good thing.

I will always remember the fun we had when the new What on Earth catalog came in the mail. We'd flip through the dozens of T-shirt designs and celebrate the ideas that came out of our own collective skulls. Plus, being able to give my children their portion of the earned creative fees was much more satisfying than handing over a weekly allowance.

The bigger lesson here might be to treat your children not like problems, but like problem-solvers. When you and I are long gone, this world will be facing challenges we can't imagine. While some political factions seem to suggest children are a burden, you can be confident that your creative, innovative kids will be part of the solution.

Choosing beauty

Eventually your conversations with your children about creativity need to acknowledge that they will have choices to make along the way. Artists can inspire and uplift, but they also have the power to demean and defile. Grade-school kids rarely think that way. But some time during their early teens, most growing artists discover they can grab some extra attention with very little effort. A blood-spattered painting. A poem about suicide. Lyrics with words they would never speak, but will readily sing.

Dad, don't panic. Know that they're flexing their creative muscles and testing boundaries. How you respond is important. I recommend you respond as a curious fan. Ask questions. Clarify what they're trying to say. In some cases, it actually might be a cry for help. But most of the time, it's a test. They're testing the power of their art. And they're testing the authority figures in their life.

In public, be an observer. In private, take a stand. Acknowledge the power of their work. Let them know they are responsible for what they create. Help them understand the difference between creating something of lasting beauty and value and the degradation of shock art. If it helps and if they can handle it, talk with your young artist about examples of so-called art that lacks any true value. That includes the infamous 1987 photograph by Andres Serrano of a crucifix submerged in urine titled *Piss Christ*, which was paid for in part by the National Endowment for Arts. Slasher movies, torture porn novels, and hip-hop lyrics that demean women are all examples of creativity that's really not very creative.

Every painting doesn't have to be filled with daisies. Every movie doesn't have to have the hero and heroine riding off into the sunset as the credits roll. Choreography should sometimes leave the dancer off balance. A symphony should include minor chords. Art should investigate and comment on the struggles of life. But if your son or daughter calls themself an artist, they have a responsibility to leave their audience glad they were witness to that art. If the audience feels like they need to take shower after attending an exhibit, watching a video, or hearing a song, the artist has failed.

The irony of nasty art

In some ways, you can't blame your child for experimenting with the dark side of their art form. Working professionals are creating tons and tons of garbage out there—and calling it art.

A vast array of today's so-called "entertainment" is violent, depressing, graphic, filthy, angry, and devoid of hope. Plus, it seems like every generation sinks to a new level of what they consider acceptable in mainstream books, movies, art, and music. Even worse than the obvious assault on our senses may be the subtle systematic perversion of our worldview. In the name of tolerance, any choice made by anyone at any time is not to be judged.

But frankly, we shouldn't be surprised. Protecting values is not the responsibility of film studios, network executives, publishers, or music producers. They are just doing their job. Their assignment is to make as much money as possible for their companies. If they don't believe in God, why would they follow a biblical worldview when pushing their products to the marketplace?

With that in mind, Dad, you need something beyond words to convince your son or daughter that there is a better option than creating more garbage, lies, and half-truths.

The answer may be found in the passage of Scripture that reads,

> Brothers and sisters, whatever is true, whatever is noble,
> whatever is right, whatever is pure, whatever is lovely,

whatever is admirable—if anything is excellent or praiseworthy—think about such things (Philippians 4:8).

Does that sound like a plan? What if we all encouraged our families to open their hearts and minds only to things that are noble, pure,
lovely, admirable, excellent, and praiseworthy?

Do such things exist? Certainly. But finding them takes work,
research, and follow-through. A dad needs to read reviews of movies,
music, and books, talk to other parents, and be a student of the culture. We need to invest a little time and money to take our sons and
daughters to fine-art galleries and uplifting concerts. Seek out quality
products from Christian artists and publishers, but also explore other
resources as well.

There's a certain irony in the fact that the human ability to create
only exists because we were made in the image of the Creator. When
artists choose to use their creative gifts to malign and blaspheme, they
are not only offending their audience, they are turning their back on
God. They're not being clever or providing witty social commentary,
they're simply revealing their ignorance. Or worse, choosing to advance
the idea that God doesn't exist.

Dads, we've got our work cut out for us. The easy answer is to cen-
sor everything. To blame the human creators of all this evil stuff and
ask our government to make it all just go away. That might be convenient, but it wouldn't help us love and give guidance to our own
young artist. Beyond just protecting them, let's equip them to battle
against it.

Which means the Bible passage above is the exact right place to start.
First, help your children open their hearts and minds to things worthy of praise. Then follow up with prayer that being exposed to such
things will lead them to discover their own beauty and value. Which
will give them confidence to create new art using their own gifts and
passions while bringing their own personal radiance. Then suddenly,
because of your children, some of the dark corners of the world will
have a few less shadows.

Questions to Get Them Talking

1. **Is it "creativity" when someone fills in the outlined images in a coloring book with a crayon?**

   Talking point: It takes tools to be creative. Imagination and decision making can happen in your mind. But the end result of creativity requires that something exists beyond yourself. An image, sound, or taste. A painting, jazz riff, or spicy jambalaya.

2. **Would photocopying a comic strip be considered art?**

   Talking point: The act of pushing a button on a photocopier is not creative. But choosing what to copy and how it will be presented could be creative.

3. **Is art useful?**

   Talking point: It inspires, motivates, calms, builds relationships, heals, causes people to think new thoughts, and so much more. Are such things useful? Consider how a piece of music or a well-acted performance elicits emotions from an audience.

4. **Can a scientist be creative? A mathematician? An accountant? A hunter? A butcher?**

   Talking point: Virtually every human endeavor requires creativity and specific performance. A skyscraper requires a solid foundation and soaring vision. Pulling a tooth requires attention to detail and a relationship with the patient. Art and science are not opposites—they are partners in just about every human activity. That's one of the things that separate us from the animals.

5. **Should art ever make an audience uncomfortable?**

   Talking point: Being creative is all about engagement. Art is meant to be talked about, argued over, and critiqued. Art should cause emotion and sometimes even discomfort. For example, many dramatic films successfully reveal the under-belly of the human condition, which leads the viewer to a new understanding. Still, there should be an inherent quest for beauty or at the very least, a desire to uncover truth. But be aware of a few recent trends. Art that's ugly. Art that's demeaning and even destructive. For example, pornography isn't art. It may be a business, an illness, a perversion, or a cry for help. But it isn't art.

Conversations to Pursue

- *Think back to when you were the age of your children.* What was your creative outlet? Did you pursue it as a career or hobby? Why or why not? Tell your kids about it. Share any regrets, but not too deeply!

- *Occasionally, your son or daughter may invite you to comment* on something they have created or a piece of creative work they appreciate. Take it in. Listen to the entire song. Examine the fabric. Look at the sculpture from all sides. Ask for time to read the entire article, script, novel, or short story. Then come back in a reasonable amount of time and use the 80/20 rule. After delivering four encouraging comments, you have earned the right to make one gentle suggestion. Especially if you are critiquing the work of a young artist, err on the side of grace.

- *In 1998, two human artists founded The Elephant Art & Conservation Project,* which features and sells "artwork" painted by elephants. The most talented of the pachyderms will hold a brush in their trunk and create abstract works of art. The humans place the empty canvases in front of the elephants that have been trained in some cases to create colorful and eye-pleasing designs including self-portraits. Is this art?

- *Genesis 1:27 tells us, "So God created mankind in his own image, in the image of God he created them."* There's much packed in those words. It describes God as a Creator and it describes humans as made in his image. Which means that we must also have the gift to create. All of us. Including you and each of your children. Dad, you are in a unique position to help your kids uncover their creative gifts. And harvest them to build God's kingdom and give glory back to him.

On Big-Picture Thinking

"My thoughts are not your thoughts, neither are your ways my ways," declares the Lord. "As the heavens are higher than the earth, so are my ways higher than your ways, and my thoughts than your thoughts."

Isaiah 55:8-9

"I've read the last page of the Bible. It's going to turn out all right."

Billy Graham

I put off replacing our garage door for several years. Structurally it was sound, but every summer the paint would blister and peel. No matter how well I scraped, sanded, or painted, it needed a new coat of semigloss white every year. Besides that, a thousand games of stickball had left the door dinged up from numerous summers of 50-mile-per-hour Wiffle balls.

It cost me $1200, but it made all the difference in the world when you pulled up to our home. Indeed, it made my bride happy and that's always a good thing. That new garage door was crisp, clean, and flawless. And I was quite certain it would stay that way. I had paid extra for a heavy-duty-grade door so the Wiffle balls would no longer leave a dent.

That's why I was quite surprised when I pulled up to the bottom of my driveway and saw what I saw. Four college-age boys—including my son, Isaac—were playing a spirited game of Wiffle ball in front of my new $1200 garage door. They had full permission to play. After all, the heavier gauge metal would nullify the chance of any dings from the pitched balls. The surprise came because my eyes focused with laser intensity on three horizontal creases in my new $1200 garage door, about eye level right behind the batter. Did I mention the door cost $1200?

You see, I had forgotten that when the batter is fooled by a pitch, his follow-through might take the broomstick all the way around in a long, wide arc. Gashing anything in its path.

Here's a question you may be wondering: *Did Jay rage?*

Allow me to claim victory on behalf of all dads everywhere. In that moment, I could have—maybe even should have—delivered an outrageous howl echoing across the entire cul-de-sac. But a couple of things happened to quench that potential outburst. First, Isaac saw my approaching vehicle, jogged down to the street, leaned into the driver-side window, and efficiently and effectively apologized. My son took full responsibility, even though, I found out later, it was his six-foot-two pal Jacob Grossman who had executed the long, arcing, damaging swing. Second, my own mind instantly saw the big picture of what was really taking place that afternoon in my very own driveway.

My college-age son and some of his lifelong friends had chosen to hang out in my front yard. No beer cans littering the lawn. No police squad cars pulling up with bad news. No video games crashing and slashing in a dark basement. These young men were playing the time-honored game of stickball. In my driveway. And I was honored. What kind of investment does that require? Broom handle: $3. Wiffle balls: $6. A garage door with stickball bruises: priceless. (Marked down from $1200.)

In the end, I came out way ahead. After all, a home is to be lived in. Dad, if you tend to stress out every time a floor gets scuffed, a table gets scratched, or a door gets dented, you're not seeing the big picture. One of your highest priorities should be to have a home in which young people feel comfortable. After they've graduated and moved up and out, there's plenty of time to repaint, resod, rescreen, and recarpet.

I have not—and probably won't—replace that wonderfully imperfect garage door. Stop by and see it next time you're in St. Charles. Think of it as a monument to big-picture thinking.

It's all good

Being in the midst of a challenging situation and knowing that everything is going to work out (a.k.a., practicing big-picture thinking) is a spiritual discipline. It's trusting God to take the sum of all our experiences and use them for good. That's a theme that arches over the entire Bible—God's promise of deliverance from darkness to light. From weeping in the night to laughter in the morning. That's a perspective we should embrace and convey to our kids.

The best-known verse reflecting that idea is Romans 8:28: "We know that God causes everything to work together for the good of those who love God and are called according to his purpose for them."

Now the one-dimensional reader might think, *Sure, it works out in the very end because all true believers go to heaven.* And that's absolutely true. That's how persecuted Christians through history and around the world today have endured the wrath of their tormentors and murderers. They know life on earth is a blink compared to eternity with God. The Bible reminds us God has prepared a place for us and we're not home yet.

But there's a second dimension to God's promise of deliverance. The Bible tells us that following God offers double value—purpose in this life and security in the next. "Godliness is profitable for all things, since it holds promise for the *present* life and *also* for the *life to come*" (1 Timothy 4:8 NASB).

In other words, put Jesus first and your life on earth finally makes sense. The joys of life are deeper because it's not just about you. You realize things like beauty, love, freedom, friendship, hope, and life itself are really a gift from the Creator. You have a relationship with God and other believers. What's more, the frustrations of life on earth—even the horrors—are filtered through a lens of confidence. You know that God will use them somehow for good.

When you're right in the middle of a tragic loss, that idea is almost impossible to grasp. Even for mature believers. Which is why we need to let our children know early and often that God can be trusted. Tell them, "Yes, life will bring frustrations and sorrow." And, "Yes, we can even be angry with God." Assure your kids that God does not turn his back on us, even when we turn our back on him. He really does have a plan for today and tomorrow. He will—somehow—make good use of every twist and turn we experience. This very moment, he sees our entire existence, and all we have to do is trust and listen.

In his book *Right from Wrong*, Josh McDowell paints a vivid word picture of how God's perspective works. Josh explains how the choices we make throughout life are like a boy stuck in a maze at a carnival. He keeps making wrong turns, getting farther and farther from the finish because from inside the maze he doesn't have enough data to make the best choices. However, when his dad climbs a tall ladder and looks down on the maze, he easily discerns the way out and guides the boy with easy-to-follow instructions, "Turn right, take the second left, follow this corridor, and so on." In other words, the dad sees the big picture.

In just this way, our heavenly Father looks down and sees all time and space—past, present, and future—at the same instant. He sees the Garden of Eden, the Garden of Gethsemane, and the herb garden in your backyard. At this very moment, he sees your first cries as a newborn, the day your own children were born, and the remarkable day when each member of your family crosses from this life into eternity. Being part of that intentional plan that stretches out as part of God's grand design should give us confidence and hope.

Applying big-picture thinking

Trusting in God's big-picture vision can rescue us from all kinds of fears, worries, and bad habits. It will make us better husbands and fathers. It will help us cope with disappointment better than any advice from a self-help guru or television talk-show host. As parents, we certainly want our children to acknowledge and understand big-picture thinking *before* they need it.

When your 16-year-old son gets cut from the high school baseball team, it's hard to watch him throw out boxes of baseball cards, favorite old jerseys, and baseball caps. In his frustration, you want to come alongside and tell him "when God closes a door, he opens a window." But in the moment, that's something you want to avoid. The risk of verbal kickback is too high. I would counsel most fathers to wait a week or longer. However, if the two of you have already embraced the idea of "big-picture thinking" and really trusting God's plan, then you can probably knock on his bedroom door and have a wonderfully encouraging conversation after only a day or two.

The same thing goes for the agony your beautiful daughter may be enduring when she gets demoted to the "B" squad, loses a coveted part in the school play to her archrival, or gets dumped by the boyfriend you never liked anyway. These kinds of nasty setbacks will happen to your little girl. Being temporarily wounded is typical and not cause for alarm. But if she knows God is in control, the recovery is quicker and less painful.

Stories—from Scripture, from your own life, and allegories—can be valuable tools to share with your children. Again, not smack in the middle of a crisis. But speak those truths into their lives way before or a little while after.

One such folktale you may want to tell involves a man shipwrecked for months on a desert island. You can spice up the story describing several failed efforts to get off the island. But the punch line is that the primitive hut he had built is destroyed in a lightning storm and the exasperated man shakes his fist at heaven. An hour later a ship pulls into the lagoon. The captain tells the astonished castaway, "We came because we saw your smoke signals." When you tell a story like this, you don't have to explain it. You can even apologize before and after and admit that it's "a little corny, but the lesson is solid."

In a true story from the Bible, Joseph's jealous brothers throw him down a well. But a passing caravan rescues him and he eventually becomes the second-most powerful man in Egypt, later saving the country and his family from famine. In the last chapter of Genesis, Joseph even tells his brothers, "You intended to harm me, but God intended it for good to accomplish what is now being done, the saving of many lives" (Genesis 50:20).

Dad, consider the disappointments, setbacks, and apparent failures in your own life. How many of them led to an open door that eventually brought significant rewards to your life? The college class you were forced to attend due to a mistake by the registrar that led to an unexpected career. The wrong turn that led to a neighborhood where you found your dream home. Look for examples from your own life of bad news followed by good news. How did you decide on a career, get your first real job, meet your wife, or find your family home? Those are stories to tell your kids. (And it's a good idea once in a while to remind yourself of God's provision.)

And what about God's angels? Psalm 91:11 promises God "will order his angels to protect you wherever you go" (NLT). You have no idea how many disasters you have missed because you were being protected. The mugger waiting down the alley you didn't enter. The job offer you didn't get at the company that was later investigated for corruption. Remember cursing that missed train, unexpected snowstorm, and alarm clock that didn't ring? Maybe your life or your reputation was being spared. Do you believe in angels? Do your kids?

God's ways are higher than ours. Let's tell our families clearly and frequently that we are glad he's in charge.

Big-picture thinking

...puts the bad stuff in perspective.
...puts the good stuff in perspective.
...is a viewpoint adults need.
...is a viewpoint we need to nurture in our children.

Through the eyes of a child

In some ways, kids see the world more clearly than we do. We see a lawn full of dandelions; they see a field of pretty yellow flowers (or puff balls to blow). We see a dilapidated cabin that doesn't quite match the photos on the vacation-property website. They see a rustic adventure with Dad.

Then there's the classic difference between how kids and adults react to mile-long freight trains. At the city's most frustrating railroad crossing, when the lights suddenly flash and the gates begin to swing down, what do dads do? For a moment we consider flooring the gas pedal and squeezing under the descending black-and-white-striped barrier. Thankfully, good sense prevails and, instead, we jerk to a sudden stop. There's no damage. Everyone's alive. Still, all that bottled-up adrenaline has to go somewhere.

Men like us have two options. We could growl, wring the steering wheel, and sit seething while 127 box cars pass ten feet in front of us. Or we could count cars. No, really. Think about it. Is a train of 127 cars good news or bad news? To grown men of wisdom and experience (like us), it's no big deal. But, to a seven-year-old in our back seat, it's huge. As a matter of fact, once the count reaches 70 or so, they're yearning to break the magical three-digit barrier. We're wishing it was over, and our kid is wanting it to go on. Your little boxcar counter will carry the excitement of 127 cars for days.

And what are you doing while they're making railroad history? You're either grumbling or leading the count. You're either cursing the lemons or making lemonade. You're either teaching your children to be optimists or pessimists. And that might be the best definition yet of big-picture thinking. Teach your kids to trust God in every situation and they'll grow to be optimistic. Model and teach them "life stinks, then you die"—and well, that's pretty much how their life will unfold.

More than just surviving setbacks

The fascinating thing about big-picture thinking is that it's not just about patience and self-control. It's about acknowledging that every cloud really does have a silver lining. You begin to count on God to work all things for good. A credit-card denial at Best Buy reminds you that you had promised yourself to cut back on TV viewing. The cable goes out, so you and the kids finally open the Settlers of Catan game you got for Christmas. You're facing ACL surgery, so you call an old friend who went through it a few years ago. His phone rings just when he needs to talk through his own personal crisis. Those aren't coincidences. That's God's plan being revealed.

When slightly bad things happen, try playing a little game with yourself and your kids. It's okay to acknowledge your frustration, but try and keep a smile on your face and figure out how to put a positive spin on the moment.

"The park district pool is closed? Let's go home and make a slip-'n'-slide. We can use a plastic tarp, dish soap, and the garden hose."

"The Prestons didn't return our tent? Looks like we're sleeping under the stars."

"A flat tire? Kids, you're about to learn a very handy life lesson on how to change a tire."

Dad, can you imagine facing most mild catastrophes and giving them each a positive spin? You just might earn yourself a reputation. When your teenagers start to say things like, "Dad! This is not good news! Why do you always have to look at the bright side of things?" that's when you know you're doing something right.

No whining allowed

One of the fabulous bonuses of teaching your kids big-picture thinking is that you now have an answer every time a child whines, screams, or mumbles, "That's not fair!"

First, of course, you want to listen to what they're really saying. It might be a legitimate concern. Your precious child might be facing some ominous threat to life or limb. You may need to step in and take drastic action. But probably not.

Most whining goes something like this:

"Tuna casserole again?"

"If a class is first period and it's raining, they shouldn't mark you tardy!"

"My room's too cold."

"My room's too hot."

"My hundred-dollar jeans don't fit right."

How should a dad respond? Without raising your voice or rolling your eyes try something like this:

"Dear child of mine. I hear what you're saying. But I hope you also hear what you're saying. You're suggesting that (blank) is causing you great misery and that you have suffered a great injustice. It's possible, I suppose. But let's look at the bigger picture. Is this injustice self-inflicted? Is there something within your own power you could change to make this tragic situation disappear? Like maybe setting your alarm clock ten minutes earlier? Or maybe you could spend a moment comparing yourself to all the other fourteen-year-old girls. Might there be some children in the world who don't even have dinner tonight? Or don't have their own room? Or have to suffer wearing jeans that are not the latest style?"

Be careful, Dad. You don't want too much sarcasm to enter into your counterattack. Your teenager may fire back with the same weapon someday. But I hope you get the idea. Big-picture thinking really does help clarify the difference between a want and a need. You absolutely should meet the *needs* of your children. But a worldview that reflects God's perspective may tone down their wants…and their whining.

Worldview as a way of life

While they're toddlers and preschoolers, you are establishing a perspective that reminds your little one about the stuff that really matters. Things like sharing, personal responsibility, obedience, God's provision, family, respect, love, and all the other character traits that flow out of big-picture thinking.

For those first few years, you are well aware of everything that feeds into their little minds. Beginning in kindergarten, however, and accelerating through elementary school, that curious mind is spending hours every day absorbing lessons and propaganda you may never know about. As much as you would like them to, teachers, coaches, and other parents won't run their worldview or life philosophies past you for your approval before presenting them to your child. Other kids bring all kinds of information and misinformation into your son or daughter's world.

How do you deal with that? First, remind yourself that the goal for each of your children is to think for themselves. All their knowledge and skill-building should *not* come from you. In the near future, they will need to take in information and accept it or reject it based on that big-picture worldview we've been talking about.

At the same time, you also need to remind yourself that your child still has a dozen more years under your care. But instead of being their sole teacher, your role has expanded. You have begun the season of fatherhood in which you take a step back and consider who your child is becoming. What are their gifts and talents? Their struggles and short-comings? Their goals and fears?

Through intentional observation, you'll know when they can fend for themselves or when they're in over their head. The goal is for your early conversations and positive reinforcements to leave them with a secure foundation to trust and even defend their worldview. Just as important, you need to establish yourself as an available mentor and sounding board for those times when they need some fresh, reliable insight. That means you need to do more listening than talking. More open-ended questions than judging. When they finally say, "What do you think, Dad?" then give them just enough opinion, backed up by just enough facts.

Phrases to use might include:

"That's a great question."

"You're on the right track."

"I don't know everything. But I know this for sure…"

"Well, there are two sides to that question. Let's look at both."

"On some issues the Bible leaves room for interpretation. But on this issue, it's pretty clear…"

As they get older, I hope you're fortunate enough to have an occasional conversation with your child that digs deep into issues that matter. It's perfectly acceptable to leave some issues on the table. When you're kicking around ideas, there may be some concepts that deserve a little more research. There may even come a time, Dad, when you say, "That's a really good point. You may be right there." But, for the most part, you need to know where you stand and why you stand there.

What you don't want to do is suggest or agree that there is no right or wrong. It's not uncommon these days for students to be taught moral relativism. College professors seem to love Friedrich Nietzsche, the nineteenth-century philosopher who infamously said, "God is dead," and who also wrote, "You have your way, I have my way. As for the right way, it does not exist."

The idea that there are no absolute truths or moral standards is the opposite of big-picture thinking. It's a small, selfish way of looking at the world. Nietzsche is saying in effect, *There is no god. There is no moral compass. It's all about me and what I want.* Feel free to ask your child if that's a world in which they want to live.

Message to dads

Every conversation you have with your child begins well before any words are exchanged. Are you pushing them away or pulling them closer? If you holler at your son for an hour about dents in the garage door, he's going to have a hard time coming to you with an even bigger personal crisis. If you dismiss your daughter's tears when she does not get asked to the homecoming dance, she's not going to open her heart to you later when she breaks up with a boyfriend who has been pressuring her for sex.

If you're building walls of judgment, they'll gladly stay outside. If you're sitting on your mountain of superiority, they won't bother to look up to you. But if you're down in the trenches, shoulder to shoulder, sharing each other's dreams and challenges, they will turn often to you for your opinion, wisdom, and experience.

Questions to Get Them Talking

1. **Does God get involved in the smallest details of our daily lives?**

   Talking point: Well, God knows exactly how many hairs are on our heads (Luke 12:7) and we are carved on the palm of his hand (Isaiah 49:15). And he's all-powerful and all-knowing, so he's capable of caring. I think he does invest in the details. Everything we do or say matters to God. Even how a kid brushes their teeth, studies for algebra, or interacts with the other kids in the school hallways. The length of your daughter's skirt? How low your son's jeans hang off his rear? God cares about all of it.

2. **Does trusting God matter more for this life or the next?**

   Talking point: This life is a finger snap compared to all eternity. So let's make eternity a priority. But, who we are right now is all we can control. Let's trust God today because we need all the help we can get. He knows what's best, right?

3. **If I gave you a candy bar now, would you eat it or save it?**

   Talking point: The ability to be patient is a huge sign that your child understands big-picture thinking. Some things are going to be difficult now, but they pay off later. It's delayed gratification. Are your kids living for today? Or have you taught them to look beyond today and beyond themselves?

4. **Why does God allow bad things to happen?**

   Talking point: That's a huge question. And that's a stumbling block for many people, and it keeps them from surrendering their life to God. The short answer is that if you know and love God, even terrible things can and will be used for good. So, from an eternal perspective, there are no "bad things." That's why we need to trust the big picture—which may not be revealed until we enter God's glory.

5. **What are some ways that God uses bad things for good?**

Talking point: Lots of ways. A delay gives you more time to think. A loss makes you more compassionate to others. A broken relationship forces you to focus on other relationships. A lost job allows you to rethink your career. Brokenness leads you to depend on God and the friends and family he has put in your life. Most tragedies make you realize that life is short and eternity is...well, eternal. Ask your older kids if they can make sense out of this quote from the second-century martyr Tertullian: "The blood of the martyrs is the seed of the church."

Conversations to Pursue

- *Tell your kids you want them to be able to come to you anytime and anyplace* with problems, concerns, and their most challenging questions. Even tougher than that is asking them if there is any reason they feel like they cannot come to you.

- *As a parent there will come times when you want to strangle and hug your kids at the same time.* For example: It's after midnight, roads are icy, your teen is way overdue, and there's no cell-phone service. They walk in the door like there's not a problem. Before your teenager gets their driver's license, talk about that scenario. In a few months, when it happens, you'll be glad you talked about it ahead of time.

- *Read 1 Corinthians 13:12*—"Now we see things imperfectly, like puzzling reflections in a mirror, but then we will see everything with perfect clarity. All that I know now is partial and incomplete, but then I will know everything completely, just as God now knows me completely" (NLT). What are the advantages and disadvantages of not seeing everything with perfect clarity?

- *It's a good thing God has limited our vision, because honestly we couldn't handle it.* Great joys and great sorrows lie ahead for all of us. They come in a flash and impact us forever. If we saw the big picture and knew everything that waited around the next corner, it would blow our minds. We'd run for cover or freeze in our tracks.

- *Are you saying "Why me, God?"* Look back at all he has done for you in the last decade. Sure, frustrating stuff happens. We might even wonder if we would be better off at our old job or even before we had kids. But God's big-picture plan is solid. Do you trust him? Do your kids?

On Work

"Without work, all life goes rotten. But when work is soulless, life stifles and dies."

Albert Camus

"Work is an extension of personality. It is achievement. It is one of the ways in which a person defines himself, measures his worth, and his humanity."

Peter Drucker

There's a plausible rumor going around that young people today are afraid of a little hard work. They don't want to get their hands dirty. They have an attitude of entitlement. They want something for nothing.

I have only anecdotal evidence, but we can speculate where the idea comes from:

- The parents of today's teenagers (you and me) are one or two generations away from the empty pantries of the Great Depression and the nationwide rationing of World War II. Growing up, we heard stories from our parents or grandparents of what it was like to actually go without something they might have wanted. Our children can't imagine opening an empty cupboard or refrigerator.

- Fewer high school kids have after-school and summer jobs. Extracurricular activities have exploded, and genuine commitment to a sport requires months of out-of-season training. Teens work long and hard at their after-school activities, which means they legitimately don't have time for employment.

- Jobs around the house—lawn mowing, painting, house-cleaning, even snow and leaf removal—are being hired out. Kids aren't expected to work and so they never learn how.

- In an attempt to make sure our kids don't feel left out or to keep up with other families, parents buy whatever their kids need or want. There's no motivation to save or get a job.

- Smaller families and divorced families are changing the financial dynamics compared to past generations.

- Technology keeps kids inside, making them only appear lazy.

What about the work ethic of your children and their friends? It's never too early or too late to launch a dialogue with your kids on the topic. If you're brave enough, plop down on the couch next to your chillaxing teen, open your Bible to Proverbs 13:4, and read, "A slug-gard's appetite is never filled, but the desires of the diligent are fully satisfied." Then politely ask, "Are you a slug or just appear to be one?"

If they're still talking with you—after that vicious attack on their lifestyle—then maybe start laying out some ground rules. Let's call them "expectations."

Pulling your weight

Just a reminder. Dad, you really should not expect your kids to get straight A's, earn first-chair violin, be elected student-council presi-dent, win a state championship, and get a full-ride scholarship to an Ivy League university. Some of those things might happen. But there are so many unpredictable factors involved that making them an expecta-tion is begging for disappointment.

But there are some things you *can* expect. Basics like brushing their teeth, turning in homework when it's due, and being ready for church on time. Common courtesies like picking up after themselves, making sure the gas tank isn't on empty after borrowing your car, and keeping you informed about their schedules. Household chores like mowing lawns, kitchen duty, and doing most of their own laundry. You can also expect them to not settle for mediocrity and push themselves to reach their full potential. That means getting involved in some worthwhile extracurricular activities, taking their own initiative to limit their screen time, volunteering in some capacity of their choosing, and setting some short- and long-term goals. In other words, pulling their weight.

For our daughter and four sons, we didn't insist they get traditional part-time jobs during their high school years as long as they were pulling down decent grades and staying involved in church and school. They did pick up babysitting, pet sitting, and landscaping jobs around the neighborhood. Other work with flexible schedules like umpiring, field maintenance, and giving hitting lessons earned them some pocket money. We didn't hand out wads of cash, but their needs were taken care of. We figured that successful high school transcripts and extracurriculars would pay off when it came time to apply to colleges.

For those four years, their "real job" was to do well in school. For each kid, you might have different expectations. The challenge is to know each child well enough that you know how hard to push and when to back off. Our five kids had the same genetic makeup, but— during their formative years—we seemed to have three natural musicians, two artists, three voracious readers, two math whizzes, two techies, three writers, one scientist, three strategic thinkers, two dreamers, and five athletes. Even as I type this, I realize that it's a mistake to slap a label on a kid and put them in a box. Still, part of your job as a parent is to help them identify and harvest their God-given gifts. Looking back, it's also amusing to see how personalities, learning styles, and passions change over the years.

One thing is sure. Kids who set their own alarm clock, have full schedules, and experience some success in some activity outside of the classroom in their teens have a strong chance of getting and holding down a decent job when they hit their twenties.

As an aside, I believe kids want to know your expectations. They want to delight you. They hate to hear your nagging, guilt trips, and ultimatums as much as you hate delivering them. But if you set reasonable expectations early and often—by example or mandate—they will respond with enthusiasm.

As you wrestle with what to expect of your children, you'll want to pull them into the conversation. Talk about giftedness, divide household tasks, prioritize expectations, coordinate calendars, and set goals for this week, this semester, and the next few years.

Work develops

...respect for Mom and Dad.
...an appreciation for the value of a dollar.
...a laboratory for future career choices.
...the satisfaction that comes from accomplishment.
...social skills as a leader, follower, and team player.

Kids want to work

Four-year-olds love to set the table, peel carrots, sweep the porch, and shovel snow. Right? So what happens between kindergarten and high school? Maybe adults take the joy out of work. We micromanage and disparage their finished product. We do jobs ourselves because it's faster with fewer mistakes. We don't take the time to instruct. Or maybe kids get the idea that work is nasty because they hear us grumbling about our bosses, co-workers, deadlines, low paychecks, and lack of job satisfaction.

It would be nice if we could all love every moment of our jobs, but that's not going to happen. At the very least, don't drag every bit of baggage from work home with you. Set a tone and standard that says, "There's satisfaction in making an honest living and providing for your loved ones."

Kids really are initially excited about tackling a new task and seeing how they measure up. But their enthusiasm can be crushed when someone says, "You don't have to do that." Or worse, "Stop doing that because you're doing it wrong."

So got a job to do around the house? Give it to the right child at the right age. If they have to stretch themselves a bit, that's great. You can even give them a wee bit more than they can handle, but not too much more. Limit their chances of failure and set them up for success. The best choice is to assign tasks that have a clear beginning and end and upon completion result in something to show for their effort. Examples of what your kid might be able do? Assemble the deck chair, seal-coat the driveway, make the salad, sweep the porch, collect the recyclables, change the baby, change all the clocks at the beginning of daylight savings time, turn the sprinkler on for one hour, stack the firewood, or paint the doghouse.

Avoid jobs that are impossible to track like "keep the ice-cube trays filled all summer long." Avoid jobs with high potential for severe criticism from Dad like "paint the front hallway." Avoid jobs with too much pressure like "proofread the speech I'm giving to the board of directors tomorrow."

The strategy is to supply them with purposeful goals and the right tools, then get out of their way. At the right intervals, you'll want to check in with them. Good questions to ask are, "Any surprises?" "Got everything you need?" and "What's your schedule for the rest of the day?" They're in charge of this task, so don't take over unless they ask for help. Also, don't be surprised if they're doing it a bit differently than the way you suggested. Let them try it their way. When they say the job is complete, don't find fault. As much as possible, say things like, "Nicely done." Later, bring it up again. Thank them for their work. Admire some aspect of their achievement.

It's amusing to consider how putting your son or daughter in charge of a necessary task might play itself out. Assign your 16-year-old the job of seal-coating the driveway and he's going to push back a little. He's watched you do it and he knows it's going to take some thought, time, and effort. He's also a little afraid of messing up. But if you know your son, he'll take ownership. When he's done, he'll brag about it to his friends. And when some grease from a buddy's pickup drips on his handiwork, your son is going to let him have it. Now that's funny.

When your child heads off into the real world armed with a solid work ethic and the ability to finish a task, they'll be rewarded with projects fit for a king. The Bible says, "Do you see someone skilled in their work? They will serve before kings" (Proverbs 22:29). Even better, they'll have you to thank.

Be an example

I may not have been the best example for my kids when it comes to establishing a consistent work ethic. The last time I punched a clock or headed off to work for a conventional 40 or 50 hour workweek was when my eldest, Alec, was nine years old. In the last two decades, my career path—weaving in and out from advertising to radio producer to author—has compelled me to work long, unpredictable hours. Some traveling. Late nights at the keyboard, which meant sleeping in the next morning. Overnight sessions with engineers in recording studios. Weekend speaking engagements. As a result, my family never had a father who systematically left home in the morning and came home in the evening. The endearing nightly exclamation, "Daddy's home!" was never chirped or cheered by my five kids.

Working for myself also meant I never really got away from client responsibilities. Never got a real vacation. And never had a steady income.

I know I'm not alone in this experience. Nontraditional working hours are not so unusual anymore. Most of the dads reading this book have gone through stages of their careers working nights, weekends, and longer hours based on the season. That includes careers in retail, agriculture, the trades, food service, hospitality, sports, entertainment, real estate, and any independent contractor.

As a dad without a "real job," my concern has always been that my children would not comprehend the idea of an adult setting an alarm, leaving for work, keeping a boss happy for a full day, and then reappearing at the front door ten hours later. I never modeled that model. Does that make me a bad dad? Would my kids stumble through life not knowing how to put their nose to the grindstone?

It turns out my kids are all out of college and productive members of society. Five different personalities. Five different career paths. All with solid work ethics. Phew.

So how does that happen? Let's list four characteristics my children might have noticed in their old dad. Ask yourself if your kids see the same values in you.

Responsibility. I didn't "go to work." But I did pay a mortgage, furnish an office, maintain the house, and sit down for dinner with my family. I hired freelance artists, engineers, voiceover talent, photographers, and video crews. I had customers and clients who counted on me and sometimes even paid their bills on time.

Communication. My family knew what I did for a living. Sort of. I would talk about clients and projects. Once in a while, I would play a radio spot or show an ad I had written. When they were younger, my wife sometimes had to remind them that "Daddy's working." Go ahead and talk to your kids about both the joys and challenges of your work. Invite them into your world for a glimpse of who you are. That increases the chance they will invite you into their world once in a while.

Respect. Your chosen career path is not nearly as important as whether you do your job well. That means staying true to your word, providing a product or service of value, delivering more than you promise, and being client-sensitive and easy to work with. A man of honor doesn't make excuses, duck responsibility, deliver shoddy merchandise, or gamble away his paycheck. Children need to see Dad as reliable and trustworthy.

Leisure. A man who works hard also knows how to play hard. There should be a time when Dad takes off his necktie or work boots and moves into "fun dad" mode. Make sure you regularly pack up the SUV and ease down the driveway for a vacation. Establish family time and keep it sacred. For several years there would be a time each week when I would finally close the door to my office and literally announce, "It's weekend." Sometimes that was Friday noon. Sometimes it was Saturday evening.

If you're a man who takes responsibility seriously, communicates well with his family, earns the respect of others, and can take time off without stressing out, then your children have a high likelihood of developing a solid work ethic of their own.

This week, ask your son or daughter to explain what you do for a living. Their answer may surprise you.

Jay's jobs

Beyond sharing your work history with your kids, share also how you got each job and why it ended. There are laughs and life lessons that will keep your family entertained for hours. My kids know my stories, and I won't bore you with all the details. But here's a brief list of my income-producing ventures beginning at age 13.

During my school years: newspaper delivery, busboy, bagger, waiter, carpenter, cotton-candy maker, boxcar unloader, and department-store Santa Claus.

My first full-time job after college was selling photocopiers to office managers in Chicago's western suburbs for the A.B. Dick Company. Then, selling law books to corporate attorneys for Matthew Bender & Company, lugging a 26-pound briefcase around Chicago's loop.

After a few death-defying years in commission sales, I heroically changed careers to become a novice copywriter for Menaker & Wright. The tiny ad agency on Chicago's famed Michigan Avenue hired me after landing the assignment from Frito-Lay to name and position what would become "Sun Chips." When that branding project finished they could no longer afford my minuscule salary. But with that experience, I landed another copywriting job at Campbell Mithun, a reputable agency with accounts like Midway Airlines, Kroger, and Corona Beer.

My fifth real job was creative director for Domain Communications, a small agency and recording studio in the suburbs that served Christian ministries and publishers. The fit was perfect, but one year later we merged with two other small agencies and the creative department moved to Seattle, leaving me without a full-time job.

My sixth job was not a job at all. For more than 20 years, I have been a freelance writer, producer, author, creativity trainer, speaker, and consultant. Dozens of clients have come and gone. And I only threaten to fire myself a couple times a year.

Looking back, I see God's hand in every one of those jobs and job changes. Like you, I gained experience and learned valuable lessons at every stop along the way. I failed some. I gained knowledge about life and about myself. I endured naysayers and leaned on mentors. Doors slammed shut. Windows opened unexpectedly.

Do your kids know about your sometimes fascinating and sometimes boring work history? That's a conversation worth having.

Their first job

Let's get real practical for a page or two. The goal is to brainstorm with your eager (or not-so-eager) son or daughter about how they can put a little spending money in their jeans and give them some experience to include when they're filling out a future college or job application. Don't show them this list. But it might inspire you to inspire them.

Lemonade stand. This classic American roadside attraction requires only a card table, chairs, cups, lemonade, hand-lettered sign, and a cash box to keep the profits. Pick a safe, visible location and a nice warm day. Remind them to smile, wave at potential customers, and serve their product ice-cold. And it's really okay if they drink all the profits.

Dog-sitting. This is a much-appreciated service around any neighborhood. When the canine member of a family is stuck at home for a long day or several days, the dog owner needs to know their pooch is not on the loose. Ask the owner to write down all instructions. And don't be surprised by anything that might happen with a cooped-up canine.

Cat-sitting. This is easy. Except sometimes the cat might hide under a table, on a shelf, or behind a sofa. Ask the owner ahead of time what to do if you can't find old Felix. On second thought, why bother? It's a cat! Who really cares about cats?

Dog-walking. Dog-washing. Dog-doo duty. If your kid loves the neighborhood spaniel or beagle, this is like getting paid for doing something you would do for free. Except for the doo-doo part.

Lawn mowing. Insist your son or daughter practices for two or three seasons on your lawn before soliciting work from the neighbors. Pretty sneaky, huh?

Babysitting. I've heard reports that good teenage babysitters are making up to a whopping $15 an hour. Your local park district may have certification classes. And hey, boys can babysit too!

Weed pulling. This might be a gardener's assistant job. Any neighbor who does their own yard work might love to have some companionship for an hour here or there. For a fee, of course.

Leaf raking. Snow shoveling. After your family shovels or rakes your own yard together, send your son or daughter on a mission. Have them ring doorbells with a rake or shovel in hand. When the homeowner asks how much, the proper answer is, "Whatever you think is fair." A thoughtful dad (that's you) will bring a bottle of water or hot cocoa out to the hardworking youngster.

You and your young teenager could probably add your own ideas depending on your part of the world. From pool cleaning to corn detasseling to clam digging. But of course, the point of all these income opportunities is not income at all. It's about helping them explore their world and take on new responsibilities. All the while you're nearby to help with any crisis management large and small.

The benefits include references, new friends, ministry opportunities, business savvy, confidence, and a new understanding of how the world works. Too many kids these days head into adulthood without some of these basic life concepts.

Think back to the very first buck you earned (not from your parents). Shoveling snow, babysitting, delivering newspapers, mowing lawns, whatever. Felt good, didn't it? Why would you deprive your young son or daughter from that same feeling?

An apprentice attitude

You've nurtured a confident kid. But that doesn't mean he or she knows everything. That may be one of the greatest challenges with young people today. Most of our brightest future stars could use a dash of humility.

Which leads us to one of the most rewarding conversations you will want to have with your child before they head off into the dog-eat-dog working world: how to be a good employee.

At school, they may be a varsity team captain, NHS president, or yearbook editor. They may have taken the lead on classroom projects, homecoming float building, and youth-group mission trips. Some day they may run their own company or congressional district. But their first job is very likely not going to need a lot of leadership skills. What their first boss does need is someone who listens and learns, shows up on time, doesn't get too creative, doesn't ask too many questions, and rarely challenges the status quo. Tell your kids that one of the most important aspects of their job is to make the boss's job easier.

In other words, have the attitude of an apprentice. You can imagine an apprentice blacksmith. His initial tasks included carrying iron, wood, and water, stoking the fire, and knowing the names of the tools. It would be months or years before he would wield the hammer, make sparks fly, and shape iron. Too many distracting questions and the job would go to a more subservient young man.

Before their first day on the job, you may want to make reference to that image of the blacksmith's apprentice in your conversation. Get your son or daughter to admit that they may not yet be an expert in flipping hamburgers, vaccinating puppies, folding cardigans for display, or club selection when the lie is in a bunker 30 yards from the pin. If necessary, explain that their IQ might very well be higher than the IQ of their new employer. But the boss' experience, title, and position with the organization means your child needs to know their place and respect authority. That's always a worthwhile lesson.

The flipside of that scenario, of course, is that your son or daughter might find themselves working alongside an invaluable mentor who invites curiosity and loves to answer questions. That boss may even give your child an ongoing series of challenging tasks that require thinking *outside the box* which helps develop new and better ways to perform critical operations leading to higher productivity for the organization for decades to come. It's possible, I suppose. But it's more likely that the only time your kids will worry about what's outside the box is when they're putting stuff inside a box to ship to Boise or Birmingham.

Dad, if your son or daughter has a few backbreaking jobs or terrible bosses along the way, that's a good thing. The two of you will have even more to talk about.

To find their own niche

Part-time jobs and summer work is one thing. A satisfying career is an entirely different animal.

How can a dad make absolutely sure his son or daughter finds lifelong fulfillment in an awesome, rewarding vocation? You can't, of course. There are far too many factors to consider.

But you are in a unique position to help them envision and stride confidently into their future. It's a delicate balance of being available and getting out of the way. It's about helping your child recognize open doors, but letting them decide whether to walk through them or not. You can help brainstorm their options, but make sure the big idea is theirs and not yours. You want to set them up for success without letting victories come too easily. You want to help them face defeat without making excuses. You want them to discover their God-given strengths and abilities and use them to serve Him. To be who God wants them to be.

Perhaps one of the best ways to guide your child is to quote Proverbs 16:3 with conviction: "Commit to the LORD whatever you do, and he will establish your plans."

Of course, each child is an individual. Kids don't come with the word *librarian, physicist, actuary,* or *Navy SEAL* stamped on their forehead. In many ways, a young man or woman is going to decide on a career through trial and error. Sometimes they will know instantly when the fit is wrong. Sometimes it takes a while. Often you might know before they do. But just as often, you need to let them play their hand until they figure it out for themselves.

The key might be for your child to throw themselves 110 percent into each of their studies and activities. When their best effort comes up short, then they know to move on to another life pursuit. In other words, encourage experimentation and discourage a slacker mentality.

Are they maximizing their efforts in every middle- and high-school subject? When they come to you and say, "French is clearly not my thing," then you can respond with confidence. "Are you putting in the time?" "Have you really given it your best shot?" "Is it just the teacher you don't like?" "Some colleges require three years of foreign language, don't they?" "If you drop French, what else would you take?"

These are all gently presented questions, not accusations or arguments. You're just helping them decide where to put their best efforts. Dad, ask lots of open ended questions and then listen. Present a question, a reliable fact, and maybe an experience from your own life. Then let them figure it out for themselves. Become an effective sounding board and they'll come to their own conclusion and they'll own that decision.

The trial-and-error process goes beyond academics. For many dads, athletics is an obvious example. But insist that your multitalented kids engage in artistic pursuits such as music, sculpture, painting, photography, or theater. Set an expectation that they need to be invested at church and see how and where they get plugged in by the youth pastor. That could reveal an entire new set of gifts and abilities. Help them find one or two additional challenging activities that fit their personality, like debate, speech, filmmaking, software or web design, sports medicine, chess, poetry, journalism, standup comedy, biblical studies, astronomy, and so on. Since there literally isn't enough time to do it all, your son or daughter will choose to drop some of these interests one by one. When the dust settles, bam! They are left with some valuable experiences and revealed talents that will lead to a successful career and ever-so-happy life.

You're going to be a what?

One final note for dads who are tempted to push your kids toward more practical careers like business, engineering, nursing, accounting, and so on. Go ahead and make your case, but leave room for other options.

What if your son or daughter is an artist at heart? Or has a legitimate chance to make it as an athlete, musician, or actor? What if their heart tells them to pursue a soul-satisfying career that is completely outside your own area of expertise? Forest ranger. Bricklayer. Archaeologist. Audio engineer.

One of the toughest things a dad must do is help open doors to careers that he just doesn't understand. Take a poll of a dozen adult friends. You will be surprised how many of them began a course of study—or remain in a career—just because they thought they had no choice. They'll say, "It's something my father wanted me to do."

Of course, they may be good at their job. It may be the exact right thing for them. But still they wonder. They have some leftover what-ifs that may never go away. (Perhaps we all have some of those.)

It's worth going back one more time to review a verse of Scripture you have very likely seen on a poster in a coach's office, dorm, or weight room. "Let us run with perseverance the race marked out for us" (Hebrews 12:1). The image on the poster probably featured some lean-muscled cross-country runner pounding pavement, sweat trickling down the side of his face.

Now you may think Hebrews 12:1 is about endurance. And you wouldn't be wrong. But did you ever consider the second half of this verse? Is there really a predetermined race course? Who marks it out? And is it just for us?

Yes, perseverance is important. Endurance. Follow through. Striving to reach the goal. But the more important thing—job one—is to identify the *right* goal. You certainly don't want your son or daughter to run with perseverance toward the wrong goal.

So Dad, pray long and hard that your child discovers the course God has laid out for them. Make sure they're well hydrated and wearing the right sneakers. Point out some of the bumps in the road, but not all of them. Establish some markers along the way—short- and long-term goals. You may even want to run alongside them for the first few miles—and then let them leave you in the dust. That's a good thing. Because that particular race isn't marked out for you, it's marked out for them.

Questions to Get Them Talking

1. **Should you get a part-time job?**

   Talking point: A kid's job is to be a kid. A high schooler's job is to get ready for the next season of life. Urge them to make the most of their high school years—to find out who God is calling them to be. A part-time job might be the best thing for some teens. They can keep their eyes open for opportunities to pick up some jobs around the neighborhood or with family friends. The best idea during those four years might be to focus on excellence in a few key areas at school. FYI: College scholarships are the only time in their entire life that they get actual cash just for being awesome.

2. **Can work be worship?**

   Talking point: Every part of our life is worship. Not just sing-
   ing in church. We're constantly giving back to God. Colos-
   sians 3:23 tells us, "Whatever you do, work at it with all
   your heart, as working for the Lord, not for human masters."
   What does that mean?

3. **Do your friends know what I do for a living? Do you?**

   Talking point: Dad, there's a good chance your own kid
   doesn't know what you do on the job. They may know the
   name of the organization you work for, but what you actually do in the course of your workday is a complete mystery.
   When Max was in second grade, someone asked him what I
   did for a living. He said, "I think he eats apples." Funny thing,
   Max wasn't too far off. Through his eyes, I'd be holed up in
   my office and, a couple of times a day, I'd come out to clear
   my head, grab an apple, and just walk around the house or
   yard. That was, indeed, a critical part of my workday.

4. **Is it okay to work on Sundays? Is it okay to bring your lap-
   top on vacation?**

   Talking point: One of the best things about work is that you
   earn the right to rest. People who never work full-time never
   experience the satisfaction of experiencing a true vacation.
   Honoring the Sabbath (the Fourth Commandment, by the
   way) is one of the ways God provides for his people.

5. **Should my work ever take priority over family?**

   Talking point: No. However, there are seasons of a career that
   require total focus and dedication. Looking back at any year,
   those days and weeks should not overshadow your responsibilities at home. Dad, don't beat yourself up if you miss an
   occasional concert, game, or event. But you do need to know
   when your child has a featured role, a solo performance, or a
   starting position for the first time. There will be some critical

events you simply cannot miss. An involved dad will know when and where he absolutely has to be. Put those dates and times on your calendar and guard them ferociously.

Conversations to Pursue

- *When you were a kid, what did you want to be when you grew up?* Did it happen? Why or why not? Are you living with regrets? Tell your kids about it.

- *Do your kids perceive different cultural expectations for men and women?* Are some courses of study and careers considered female and some male? Are men still expected to be the breadwinner in the family? Is it acceptable or preferable for moms to stay home with the kids?

- *Can a woman (or a man) find personal fulfillment* staying home, cooking dinner, raising children, volunteering at school and church, and managing a household while their spouse earns the bulk of the income?

- *There's an old saying: "Do what you love and the money will follow."* Is it important to love what you do for a living? Is money important? What's more important than money?

- *A word to T.G.I.F. dads.* If your work is total misery 50 hours per week and you only live for weekends, you may be sending the wrong message to your kids. Of course, there are aspects of all jobs and careers that are not fun. With older kids, that's a great point to cover. But if you hate everything about your current job, please don't drag that misery home with you.

- *Read Genesis 2:15.* "The LORD God took the man and put him in the Garden of Eden to work it and take care of it." Even in paradise, God expected man to work. That's something to think about.

Conversation 6

On Money

"Money never made a man happy yet, nor will it. The more a man has, the more he wants. Instead of filling a vacuum, it makes one."

Benjamin Franklin

"I've got all the money I'll ever need, just so long as I die by four o'clock."

Henny Youngman

I'm on record insisting that family, friends, readers, acquaintances, neighbors, and even my kids should not take financial advice from me.

I do quite a few things well. Financial planning is not one of them. My rainy-day savings have either washed away or dried up. My 401-K is not okay. And I certainly cannot count on my employer for any kind of substantial pension plan, because I'm self-employed.

On the math portion of the ACT, I scored in the top 1 percent. Really, I did. But having a mathematical mind does not necessarily translate to financial savvy. Just like being an English major doesn't mean your son will write thank-you notes without a reminder. And being a whiz at technology doesn't mean your daughter will remember to set an alarm clock.

With that caveat, allow me to share a few financial truths I have learned the hard way—and then offer some ways to pass those truths on to your kids. You already know that debt, savings, cash flow, budgets, and overspending are issues that can bring a family together or drive them apart.

Get on the same page with your bride

Whether you're a married dad or a single dad, you won't be surprised to hear that experts say "finance" is the #2 cause of marital and family discord. It doesn't matter how much money is coming in. There always seems to be unexpected expenses that blow the budget (if there is a budget). And there's quite often a difference of opinion about what's important. All of us like to keep up with the Joneses. Some of us, unfortunately, are driven to keep *ahead* of the Joneses.

Are you enduring an ongoing "frugal vs. prodigal" conflict? Sometimes arguments about money are loud and frequent. Sometimes— and maybe this is even worse—opinions on financial priorities remain unspoken and hidden just below the surface. Conventional wisdom suggests that women are the spenders and men are the savers. But that can easily change with the seasons of the year and the seasons of life.

Your wife may have an addiction to shoes, mani-pedis, Coach purses, or five-dollar coffees that burdens your budget like clockwork. Thinking about her impulse purchases, you grit your teeth, but you're out of ideas on how to gently break the habit. You, on the other hand, carefully watch all your nickels and dimes month after month, year after year. Then one day you come home with a $12,000 snowmobile or $75,000 Maserati. That's not just a bad habit. That's a midlife crisis.

It doesn't matter who speaks first. You both know that a conversation needs to take place and a plan needs to take shape. One of you needs to have the courage to say, "It cannot go on like this." And the other needs to have the courage to say, "Let's face this together." Unspoken pressure builds on both sides, so you'll want to approach that kind of meeting with sensitivity, wisdom, love, and trust. The goal is not to point fingers or assess blame. Nor should you expect to come up with a perfect plan that lasts for decades in one sitting. The takeaways from any financial planning powwow need to be 1) we're in this together, 2) we could both make some adjustments, and 3) once we get a handle on this, we'll celebrate together. If you can finish the challenging conversation with a kiss and a cuddle, even better.

By the way, don't be surprised if an open and honest conversation—bringing all your financial concerns out into the light—takes a huge burden *off* your marriage. Early in our marriage, I was working on commission selling A.B. Dick photocopiers door-to-door in office buildings. It was never pleasant telling Rita that my commission check was not going to be very impressive the upcoming month. That was when Rita starting hiding bills from me, which is never a good idea. Even though the news was unpleasant, getting it out in the open was always a relief.

In similar fashion, if there's any issue that's causing your children to lose sleep or lose connection with you—whether it's about money, grades, friends, bad habits, the future, or whatever—get it out on the table. Some issues are close to terrifying. And you might not like everything you hear. But done with love and respect, opening the floodgates to reveal what's really going on is the beginning of healing and hope. And as described above, if you can finish those conversations with a kiss and a hug, even better.

Getting to the heart of the matter is the goal. Working through agonizing financial conversations and finally being on the same page is worth the open heart surgery. I absolutely believe that getting through those early days—together—is one of the reasons Rita and I are so much in love today.

Warnings and lessons

Here are a few general rules of thumb that even a financial bonehead like me can understand. At the right time—especially when they get their first real full-time job—pass them on to your kids either with clear specific words or by example.

- If your place of employment offers some kind of automatic payroll saving deduction, do the maximum amount. Especially if they offer matching funds.

- If you haven't yet, start some investment with your very next paycheck. Even if it's just twenty bucks. You may think the money manager or investment counselor is going to laugh at a measly investment, but they won't. Everyone starts small.

- Buy slightly used cars and pay cash if at all possible. (Also, find a good mechanic you can trust.)

- The only thing you should really borrow money for is a house. Everything else you should only buy if you have money in hand.

- Get a 15-year mortgage.

- Splurge rarely. Be frugal in spending 95 percent of the time, so that when you splurge, it's special! If you go out for steak and lobster every week, it loses its deliciousness.

- It's okay to use credit cards for convenience, but pay them off every month. I repeat. Pay them off every month.

- Never, ever be late with a credit-card payment. They will jack your interest rate up to 20, 25, even close to 30 percent.

Did I mention that many of the above principles were learned the hard way? Well, Dad, you can be sure of this. You can model, talk, urge, and suggest all day long to your kids about financial matters. Hopefully, you'll rescue them from some of the nastiest pitfalls. But you should expect that some things, they too will learn the hard way. If you're lucky, they may come back and say, "Dad, you were right." But don't hold your breath.

Money:

…is the central point of conflict in most court cases and family disputes.
…doesn't last.
…is a tool that should be used carefully and wisely.
…is not a good reason to marry.

Point to the "Prodigal Son"

Some of the best conversations you have with your kids revolve around stories of when you were their age. Your mind-numbing morning paper route. Your embarrassing buck teeth and braces. Your days riding the bench in the dugout. Your failed attempt at changing and gapping spark plugs.

And you do tell great stories! But sometimes they get repetitious. And maybe a little preachy. In some cases, you may not have any specific personal stories about issues you want to share with your kids. Which means you need other stories and truths to point to. Consider opening your Bible to Luke 15.

Theologians would typically say Jesus' parable known as the "Prodigal Son" is about God's unconditional love and how he will always celebrate the day when a lost person finally surrenders to grace. We looked at that parable back in chapter 1, "On Family." But there's also a nice subplot about how money issues can wreak havoc with family relationships.

The bratty little brother demands a big cash inheritance from dad who—for some reason—gives in. The kid blows every nickel partying with strangers. When the money is gone the friends don't stick around. Surprise, surprise. While the prodigal is yearning for pig food, he finally comes to his senses and heads home.

In the meantime, the older son is now stuck doing twice the work and has zero cash in his pocket. Then, when the twerpy little brother comes over the hill, Dad runs out, gives him a big hug, and throws a blowout bash! Does that sound fair? Ask your kids what they think!

Among all the other lessons in this great parable are a bunch of lessons on money that might speak volumes to your children of different ages. One thought is that your children should be able to come to you for anything. Of course, you might say no and you might say yes. Second, "wild living" burns up money pretty quickly. Third, you can't buy friends. People who hang around because you've got a fat wallet are not real friends. Fourth, famines come and go. Be ready. Fifth, it's no fun being hungry, so learn a skill and don't be afraid to get dirty. Sixth, hard work never hurt anyone; plus it gives you time to think. Seventh, some people have to hit bottom to really appreciate the stuff that really matters. Avoid that, if possible. Eighth, Mom and Dad's door is always open. Ninth, it takes time to fatten up a calf, but it's nice to have one when you have something to celebrate. Tenth, at one point, the father says to the older son, "Everything I have is yours." That's a nice thing to say to your kids. It's comforting and empowering. Don't worry, they probably won't instantly insist on their percentage of the trust fund. But you do want your kids to know that you intend to give them everything they need. (Which is different than giving them everything they want.)

Wow. You didn't know all those financial lessons were in one little parable, did you?

Point to the time Jesus raged

Popular culture has this image of Jesus being a really sweet guy who would never be judgmental or express any anger whatsoever. But that's not the Jesus of the Bible. The Son of God took a stand when it came to sinners, blasphemers, and those who would divert him from his earthly mission. He cried, "Woe to you, teachers of the law and Pharisees, you hypocrites!" (Matthew 23:13). Jesus' judgment continued against those who would bring harm to a child. He warned, "It would be better for them to be thrown into the sea with a millstone tied around their neck than to cause one of these little ones to stumble" (Luke 17:2). When Jesus predicted his own death, Peter protested the plan. Jesus strongly rebuked him: "Get behind me, Satan!" (Mark 8:33).

Jesus' most public and notable recorded outburst was all about money. Merchants and moneychangers had set up shop in the temple, charging exorbitant fees and crowding out those who came to worship.

> Jesus entered the temple courts and drove out all who were buying and selling there. He overturned the tables of the money changers and the benches of those selling doves. "It

is written," he said to them, "'My house will be called a house of prayer,' but you are making it 'a den of robbers'" (Matthew 21:12-13).

When you find yourself talking with your children about the idea that Jesus was both fully God and fully man, point out the times he got angry. And throw in a lesson about how Jesus made it clear that God is who we worship, not the almighty dollar.

Point to the fate of lottery winners

Here's a guaranteed opportunity to talk about healthy money strategy with your children. Whenever the regional or national lotteries promise a giant cash payout, you can be sure a TV news reporter will visit some sleazy mini-mart, shove their microphone into the face of someone waiting in line to buy a ticket, and ask, "What would you do if you won the jackpot?" Feel free to turn to your son or daughter and say that you feel sorry for those folks in line.

First, they're putting their hope in something that doesn't last. Even if they won, millions of dollars doesn't last into eternity. Why, it doesn't even last here on earth! It's easy to find stories of lottery winners who eventually declare bankruptcy. The National Endowment for Financial Education estimates that up to 70 percent of Americans who experience a sudden windfall lose that money within a few years.

Second, tell your children that anyone who wins the lottery is missing out on the satisfaction of earning their rewards the old fashioned way—through hard work and savings. It's no surprise that young people are looking to make a quick killing. Rumors abound about college dropouts who became millionaires through Internet, real estate, or other get-rich-quick angles. Make sure your children know how easy it is to fall prey to con men, pyramid schemes, and web-based scams. Proverbs has a great bit of wisdom to pass on anytime kids start talking about making easy money, "Wealth from get-rich-quick schemes quickly disappears; wealth from hard work grows over time" (Proverbs 13:11 NLT).

Point to the 2300 Bible verses about money

The Bible has some 500 verses concerning faith and about 500 on the topic of prayer. But more than 2300 on money and possessions. Here are just a few:

> Whoever loves money never has money enough; whoever loves wealth is never satisfied with their income (Ecclesiastes 5:10).

> Keep your lives free from the love of money and be content with what you have, because God has said, "Never will I leave you; never will I forsake you" (Hebrews 13:5).

> The love of money is a root of all kinds of evil. Some people, eager for money, have wandered from the faith and pierced themselves with many griefs (1 Timothy 6:10).

> Where your treasure is, there your heart will be also (Luke 12:34).

What do you love? Who is your master? Where is your treasure? In our culture, money has a stranglehold on most guys. Even worse, our children are mimicking our focus on making more money and acquiring more stuff. When you envision success for your kids, do you envision a well-paying job with a big house? Or do you visualize your grown children with a strong faith and humble, grateful hearts?

Point to the undiscovered opportunities

Looking back on the more than 30 years of marriage, I recall dozens of times when God nudged me, "Jay, this is something you should do." Way too many times, I had full awareness of the opportunity before me, but had to say no because I didn't have the funds. What a shame. I do believe it's a biblical principle that when he opens a door, God also provides the funds, manpower, and timeline. In those instances when I didn't follow through, maybe my faith was weak. Or maybe *not* doing it was God's plan. It's even possible I endured those regrets so I could pass this wisdom on to you. So here it is: get your financial house in order, so that when God opens a door, you can walk through without hesitation.

Point to the privilege of tithing

The concept of giving 10 percent of your income back to the Lord goes back to the Old Testament and is rooted in the fact that God should be first in our lives. Right off the top, we give our firstfruits back to him.

> Be sure to set aside a tenth of all that your fields produce
> each year (Deuteronomy 14:22).

I hope you have embraced the rewarding and worshipful habit. Even if you're not doing the exact math, I hope you're investing sacrificially in God's work. If so, the question for today is, "When did you start tithing?" Very likely you were an adult and it took an eye-opening message, a heart-to-heart conversation with your wife, and some real soul-searching. Good for you! Since then, you have undoubtedly seen God's blessing pour into your lives in unexpected ways. Maybe not financially, but you've settled into a more contented life and gained some new freedoms. Tithing is a gift from God.

The follow-up question then is this: "When and how will you begin to encourage or challenge your own children to tithe?" With their summer jobs, babysitting and lawn-mowing money, and weekly allowance, shouldn't they be tithing so they can experience all the blessings of God's plan for our worldly wealth?

The earlier you start, the easier it is. It's pretty hard to say, "Hey, burger-flipping son. You know that $132.70 paycheck you earned by sweating over a hot grill in a ridiculous-looking uniform? Well, now you must put exactly $13.27 in the collection basket this Sunday." That's probably the exact wrong approach. As a matter of fact, he'll probably start asking his burger-joint manager to schedule him on Sunday morning shifts so he has an excuse to avoid the passing of the basket.

A better plan might be for you to model your own cheerful giving and make sure your teenager's basic financial needs are being met. Then, make a clear statement *before* that first paycheck even arrives. (Maybe even as the teenager *begins* the job search.) Consider giving a little speech. Something like, "Your first job. That's kind of exciting. You're entering a new world and you'll do well. I'm proud of you. But let me tell you one of the biggest surprises when that first paycheck comes. On the stub, you'll see a bunch of little boxes that say things like FICA, state income tax, federal income tax, social security, and maybe some others. It's all money coming right out of your pocket. Paying for government services is all part of chasing the American dream. Welcome to adulthood. When your first check comes, bring it to me and we'll see if I can decipher some of those deductions.

"On the other hand, one of the best parts about having a little income is being able to give some of it back to God. He gave you the ability to think, work, and be productive. So really, everything is his anyway. Be glad he's letting you keep most of it. I'm not going to tell you how much to give or even who to give it to. That's between you and God. But every week or every month, you're going to want to invest in his work. It could be supporting a friend going on a mission trip, sponsoring a child through Compassion International, or putting five or ten percent in the collection plate on Sunday. It's something to pray about. I gotta warn you. It's going to feel good. Like you're part of something bigger than yourself. But don't do it for the feeling. Do it because it's the right thing to do."

When that first paycheck comes, don't make another big speech. I recommend you joke about how now they can buy all their own clothes, pay for their own schoolbooks and extracurricular fees, and take you out to dinner real soon. When they groan—or laugh in your face—tell them you were just kidding. But then quickly add, "I know you've got all kinds of ways to spend that big fat paycheck. And some will be totally wasted. That's probably okay. But in the long run, your best bet is to save 20 percent, tithe 10 percent, and just be smart with all the rest. That actually sounds like a good plan for every bit of income you get for the rest of your life."

Use this parenting trick

Proverbs 21:20 says, "Fools spend whatever they get" (NLT). Now, I'm not calling your kid a fool, but there's a good chance that if you give your son or daughter twenty bucks for an outing or field trip, they're going to spend every nickel. Any parent of a middle schooler would not be surprised by that.

I ran across a practical lesson on countering this mentality in an article from Jonathan Clements, wealth-management consultant and former columnist for the *Wall Street Journal*. The best part of this strategy is you don't have to lecture. They learn the principle all by themselves.

The basic idea is to "make your kids feel like they're spending their own money." When your nine-year-old goes on a class field trip, you expect them to ask you for lunch and spending money. Dutifully, you peel a ten or a twenty out of your money clip. But don't just give it to them and say, "Have a good time." They'll gladly spend your hard-earned cash and you will have reinforced the perception that money grows on trees. Also don't say, "Bring me back the change." They'll keep spending that day until it's gone and you'll be lucky to get back 37 cents. Instead, look them in the eye and say, "This is now your money. It's my gift to you. Whatever you don't spend on the field trip is yours for something you may need or want later. Have a great time. I want to hear all about it when you get home." At the cafeteria your sharp child will dine sensibly. When they get to the museum gift shop, they'll think twice before buying the dust-collecting plastic dinosaur or the genuine artificial Native American tomahawk made in China.

If they save a few bucks that's great. If they blow it all that day, there's a good chance they'll have a twinge of regret and come away with a real-life lesson.

Putting money in perspective

For now, U.S. currency says, "In God We Trust." That's our government—believe it or not—giving some pretty good advice. One interpretation could be that every time we hold a coin or piece of currency, we should remind ourselves that God should have more impact on our lives than money.

Still, money seems to dominate most of our life decisions. Any lengthy conversation about work, vacations, retirement, cars, entertainment, traveling sports, buying a house, choosing a college, or even how many kids to have is going to include the topic of money. How to make more of it. How to spend less of it. Saving it. Wasting it. Giving it away.

Dad, when you're having those conversations as a family, you need to make every effort to not make money the driving force in your decision making. If you make money your master, it will quickly rule every decision you make.

You know Matthew 6:24, "No one can serve two masters. Either you will hate the one and love the other, or you will be devoted to the one and despise the other. You cannot serve both God and money."

That's a verse you can pull out anytime the conversation turns to the almighty dollar. But don't stop reading there. The rest of that chapter talks about how God cares for each of us and how we shouldn't worry so much about what we're going to eat and what we're going to wear. Chasing stuff and agonizing about the future is what nonbelievers do. Matthew 6:33 says, "Seek first his kingdom and his righteousness, and all these things will be given to you as well."

Admittedly, this entire issue is difficult and even a little confusing for dads. We want our kids to get well-paying jobs. To buy a nice house. To be able to dress and feed our grandkids. And take nice family vacations. In short, fathers want their children to be successful.

But that's the point. Dad, lead your family to God's kingdom and righteousness, and—as our heavenly Father—he's going to make sure you and your kids have everything they need.

Questions to Get Them Talking

1. **Would you rather win the lottery or know you have a reserved spot in heaven?**

   Talking point: It should be a no-brainer. If your kid says, "Win the lottery," then quickly point out the flaw in their answer by comparing our brief moment on earth to all of eternity. Really, questions like this help cement their worldview. A more tangible version of this question might be, "Would you betray your best friend for a thousand bucks?" Your kids already know that relationships are more important than money, but sometimes they forget what that means.

2. **Is money important? What's more important than money?**

   Talking point: Don't deny the importance of money. But make sure they see it as a tool we can use to build God's kingdom. The list of things that is more important than money should include things that aren't really for sale. Open your Bible to the fruit of the Spirit and you'll find a nice list to share with your children. That's Galatians 5:22-23.

3. **Where should we invest our end-of-the-year gift?**

   Talking point: You may not want to talk about specific amounts, because that may come back to bite you. "Oh, fine—you can give $500 to dig wells in Africa, but you can't give me $20 for pizza with my friends." But let your kids know that every Christmas you make a gift to a favorite charity. Invite them to make suggestions. Or make a short list of potential projects and let them vote. Maybe even invite them to contribute.

4. **Which of the commandments are about money?**

   Talking point: Commandment #5? "Honor your father and mother." Sure, children need to appreciate how parents provide for them. How about Commandment #7? "You shall not steal." Obviously. Commandment #10? "You shall not covet your neighbor's house…" Of course. But don't forget about Commandment #2: "You should not make for yourself an idol." That's all about putting money ahead of God.

4. What's the best way to keep money from being our god?

Talking point: Give it away! In the grand scheme of things it's not really yours anyway. It's on loan. You can't take it with you. Once you've mastered the art of giving, take another more dramatic step. Try giving *in secret*, generously, magnanimously, and without telling anyone or expecting anything in return. Keep it just between you, your kids, and God.

Conversations to Pursue

- *The world often misquotes the Bible.* One example: The Bible never says, "Money is the root of all evil." First Timothy 6:10 says, "*The love of* money is the root of all evil." (FYI: The Bible also never says, "God helps those who help themselves," "Charity begins at home," or "A fool and his money are soon parted.")

- *If God is going to take care of our every need, why should we plan for the future?* Or save? Or even work? Also, why should we give to those who are less fortunate? Won't God take care of them? A few responses you need to have ready are ones like these: "Meeting your needs is a promise from God, so ask yourself how he has gifted you to meet your own needs." "When it comes to the needs of others, we are often the tools God uses to make a difference." "Our job is to listen for God's call and be ready to serve. If possible that means to stay healthy and have the resources to respond."

- *Look for lessons in sharing.* Little kids love the plastic trinkets, balloons, candy bits, and other knickknacks they win at school fairs and church picnics. As a dad, you don't want to mock their natural accumulation of those treasures. Saying, "You don't need that junk," doesn't really make any point at all, except that Dad is no fun. But if your child wins a bounty of that worthless loot, maybe you can create a teachable moment at the next silly Saturday event. Seek out a smaller child (or less competitive child) walking around with empty arms, and navigate your own child into position so they see what you see. It could be a great lesson in sharing.

- *How do you reply if your child ever suggests that another family is lucky* because they have a bigger house, better cars, more extravagant vacations, and so on? Well, you could brainstorm on how to bring more money into the family. Suggest things like overtime for Dad, Mom goes back to work full-time, junior gets a job, sell that second car, cancel the life and health insurance, stop tithing, or get rid of the dog. Suddenly the decisions are not that easy. Don't exhaust your kids by putting them in charge of family finances, but they need to know that you've put many hours of thought and prayer into your budget.

- *I hope there were days early in your marriage in which you felt totally broke.* Now that you have kids, you're about to discover one of the reasons God brought you through that time of discouragement and fear. Those memories of how God provided make great stories to tell the next generation. If you were never that broke, then sorry, you missed out on an experience that would have strengthened your marriage and family.

- *Let your kids know early you will do what you can* to help pay for college and their other educational needs. But there are tons of things they can do also. Keep their grades up. Be active in extracurricular activities. Build good relationships with teachers, coaches, school administrators, and counselors because they can be very helpful along the way. Keep open to multiple options when it comes to courses of study. Apply for grants and scholarships. Dad, do everything possible to prevent your kids from graduating college with the burden of huge student loans.

Conversation 7

On Laughter

"There are souls in this world who have the gift of finding joy everywhere, and leaving it behind them when they go."
Frederick William Faber

"You don't stop laughing because you grow old. You grow old because you stop laughing."
Michael Pritchard

Years ago I attended a parenting seminar featuring some guy billed as an "internationally known expert." For an hour, I watched him wring his hands, point fingers, agonize, accuse, and yell about the importance of reasserting parental authority and keeping your kids in line. Not once did I hear him talk about *the joy of fatherhood.*

The speaker had a few memorized jokes, but the punch lines all seemed to center on how kids are "more trouble than they're worth." He relentlessly insisted that today's teenagers and parents could not possibly have a civil adult conversation about life, current events, weekend plans, college plans, friends, hopes, or dreams. He characterized parenting as "us" against "them." This so-called international expert presented parenthood as years of gruesome, torturous, thankless toil.

Does that describe your attitude toward parenting? I hope not. And by now, I hope you also are well aware that one of my goals is for my home—and yours—to be filled with unconditional love, engaging communication, and lots of laughter.

What kind of laughter? Belly laughs. Chuckles. Chortles. Giggles. Guffaws. And cracking quiet smiles. But the end goal is not just laughter. The goal is for your home to be welcoming and user-friendly. The goal is for members of your family (including you, Dad) to be drawn to this warm, wonderful sanctuary. A place overflowing with love and joy.

In that kind of home, kids are not the enemy. They are partners in merrymaking. When they're down, you pick them up. And vice versa.

The key driving force behind that kind of relationship is…well, relationship. The more time you spend with each other, the more you know what tickles each other's funny bone. Some folks (guys) like the slapstick buffoonery of the Three Stooges. Some folks appreciate puns, malaprops, and other wordplay. A large segment of the population appreciates the witty scripted dialogue of light comedy. That's why network executives continue to develop laugh-track-enhanced situation comedies based on a small group of people in, obviously, a relationship—families, friends, co-workers. Some sitcoms might even be worth a half hour of your life once a week. Most probably not.

The latest generation of these shows often goes too far with sexual innuendo and vulgarity that is far from clever. Still, there is some thoughtful, well-produced programming available for discerning viewers.

As an aside, let me mention that television opens all kinds of doors to conversations with your children. When your nine-year-old asks if they can turn on the television, it's perfectly acceptable to ask, "What's on?" If they confirm that a favorite show is about to air or has been recently recorded, then you have the perfect opening to gain valuable information about their viewing preferences. "I've heard about that show. What's the premise?" There's also a high likelihood they don't actually have a viewing plan and just want to channel-surf. You always have the option, Dad, of saying, "There's got to be a better use of your time." But once in a while, go ahead and plop down next to them on the sofa and say, "I have an hour to kill, let's see what we can find." Once in a while, it's wise to watch what they watch. Whether it's great or awful, you've got a foundation for lively conversation, guidance, and debate—and maybe an ongoing laugh or two.

Other not-so-uplifting genres of humor include trash talk, sarcasm, satire, practical jokes, and potty humor. A little might be fine. But a little also goes a long way. Sometimes too far. It's like when the baby burps at the dinner table. Brother, sister, Mom, and Dad can't help but laugh. And that's a good thing! But when the older kids follow up with their own version of dining-room belching, it's not nearly as funny. You can't punish them, but you need to let them know that comedy requires discernment. Comedy works best within boundaries.

When my kids were young, I came up with a three-word phrase that you might want to utilize. Get them quiet and say, "That's enough. Once is funny." Those words—"Once is funny"—get everyone off the hook. You've still had a good laugh together, but when you don't laugh the second time, you're not being hypocritical. You're just demonstrating adult restraint.

In the same way, some practical jokes are amusing, but most are not. Sarcasm is a bad idea 98 percent of the time. Sure, a little trash talk can add spice to a game of driveway basketball with your middle-schooler. *"Boo-yah. Three for me." "Stop, drop, and roll...I'm on fire." "You just got spanked by your old man."* But be prepared for the day when you get schooled at the driveway hoop by your own son or daughter. And remind them often that trash talk has no place in organized sports. Reserve it for friendly pickup games only; even then handle with care.

Dad, I recommend you declare yourself to be keeper of comedic boundaries. As a way to define how far is too far, you may want to keep these phrases handy:

"Once is funny."

"This court is a trash-talk-free zone."

"You don't need to put that kind of stuff in your head."

"Guys, how is that funny? It actually seemed kinda mean."

"That's rated R, isn't it? Son, did you really have to ask? We're going to hold off on the R-rated movies a few more years. Okay?"

"It's too bad about that comedian. He used to be clever. Now he's using potty humor to go for the shock value and easy laughs."

"On Netflix tonight, let's try classy instead of trashy."

One verbal-boundary warning that always perplexed me was when a guy says, "Watch your language. There's a lady present." In my mind, if a word or phrase is inappropriate, it's inappropriate. For guys and gals. Or maybe that's just me.

On the other hand, "Watch your mouth, there are kids around," seems to make sense. Adults can filter words and ideas that kids cannot. With that in mind, go ahead and talk with your older kids about whether or not it is ever appropriate to use "adult language." Be specific. Decide if there is ever an acceptable time to use "damn," "crap," or "pissed off." You might want to recommend, "dang," "crud," or "ticked off." Even including the previous words in this manuscript might be a poor choice. It's worth talking about.

Start early

No matter what age your kids are, see if you can make them laugh today. The older they are, the more challenging it gets. Got a baby? It's easy. And it's healthy for them. And you.

Beginning at one day old and for the next few years, here are just a few laugh-inducing techniques to use with your kids. Whisper, "Hello. This is your daddy." Stroke their little cheeks. Scrunch your nose. Gently sing old pop tunes. Rub their tummy. Quack. Moo. Howl. Growl. Cluck. Kiss their toes. Burble their belly. Make silly faces at them. Make silly faces with them in a mirror. Play peek-a-boo. Play "guess which hand." Roll them balls. Tickle them gently. Put non-hat items on your head. Tell them they have "stinky feet." Use funny voices. Pretend to cry. Play monsters. Talk gibberish. Call your nose an ear or call your ear a nose. Rhyme everything. Imitate them. Sing nursery rhymes. Sing nursery rhymes but mess up the words. Jump on the bed. Pillow fight! Read a book upside down. Play hide-and-seek. Give noogies. Tell knock-knock jokes. Introduce puns. Hold staring contests. Dance in the kitchen. Be a goofball.

That's all a good start. But then beware. Right around second grade, kids start the unsavory and almost unstoppable practice of gross-out humor. As the father of four boys, I cannot endorse potty humor or gross-out shenanigans in any way, shape, or form. So I will not be telling you about any sculptures sitting on a fencepost made from dog poop or one brother chasing another brother around the basement with dirty underwear.

And I will certainly never tell you about the time four boys were left in the minivan while Mom went into the print shop to pick up PTO flyers and how 12-year-old Alec convinced 6-year-old Max that in an emergency it was okay to pee in a Coke can. And I especially would never confirm that the nice lady who carried the box of flyers out to the minivan offered to take the Coke can, saying with a hint of pride, "I'll take that. We recycle." And I will deny that when those boys—now all college grads—are together, if someone says, "We recycle," they laugh like they were still in elementary school.

All that to say, if you want to laugh with your kids, you need to know your audience. Spending time with them is the only way to know what tickles their fancy.

Have lots of kids

Rita and I had five. Plus we've had the great privilege to love on ten additional foster babies. Now, I am certainly not going to tell you how many kids to have. But when I speak to parents' groups, I look out and see wonderful eager faces of men and women who love their kids and want to be the best moms and dads they can be. And sometimes I can't help myself, so I give a little speech:

"If you're considering it at all, have more kids. The world needs more great families with great kids. Maybe you've heard some naysayers argue that there are already too many people on the planet. Well, I'm looking around and I can tell that your children are not part of the problem. Your children are part of the solution. Talk it over with your spouse. But consider

*making another baby or two. Or adopting. After all, you'll need kids to take
care of you in your old age. And I need your kids to pay into Social Security."*

I don't know if my little light-hearted rant has caused even one
more baby to be born, but I hope so. I've seen in my own family that
when there are more kids in a room or sitting around a table, the chance
for laughter increases exponentially. Everyone has a bad day once in a
while, right? With seven of us hanging out together, there was always
at least one or two of us having a good day. If you let it, that positive
vibe can spread from one person to the next and pretty soon everyone
is on the right track. Even when both Rita and I were having a rough
time, a few minutes with a silly six-year-old or an appreciative eighth-
grader could almost always turn things around.

When Alec and Randall began edging toward adulthood, an even
more amazing thing happened. As busy high school upperclassmen
and college students, those two boys would still make time for their
younger siblings. If Max, Isaac, and Rae Anne had a problem or question to work through, they didn't necessarily come to Mom or Dad. I
watched from a distance and saw earlier conversations and debates that
I had with the older boys being replayed to the younger kids. In other
words, the time invested in the older boys was reaping additional profit.
Never was anyone feeling abandoned and alone with a life challenge.
Because burdens were shared, there was a sense that "more kids" was
easier than "fewer kids."

Believe it or not, that also applies to the family cash flow. Logic
might suggest that having five kids would cause the budget to be tighter
than with smaller families. But it probably made little difference. If we
were raising just one or two children, there would have been more din-
ners out and fancier vacations. You can't put a price tag on a home filled
with laughter. In those years when the bills were piling up, more than
a hundred times I said to Rita, "Well, they can take our house and our
cars, but they can't take our kids."

If you didn't know it—kids are a gift. Their purpose is to bring
joy and blessings. I am continually touched by the last few lines of
Psalm 127:

Children are a gift from the LORD;
    they are a reward from him.
Children born to a young man
    are like arrows in a warrior's hands.
How joyful is the man whose quiver is full of them!

Men, you probably know the long pouch on the back of an archer that holds his arrows is called a quiver. And if you have a full quiver—lots of kids—you have a great shot at a life filled with joy.

Now, I'm not sure if you've ever tried quiet meditation. But Psalm 127 provides an image on which you could meditate for quite a while.

You're an archer. You are young, strong, and confident. You reach over your shoulder and extract a single arrow from your quiver. You crafted that arrow with care and packed that quiver yourself, so you know the shaft is straight and true, the feathered fletching precise. Still, you slide your fingers down the narrow cylinder in preparation for a flawless fight. You've spent many hours disciplining yourself, and so it feels natural to slide the notch of the arrow onto the bowstring. Combining strength and gentleness, you pull that arrow toward you. Close to your heart. With great care you choose a target that's exactly right for this exact arrow. You remain steadfast, feet planted firm. With a slight smile you let the beloved arrow fly. Your assignment as warrior is complete.

That was so much fun. You do it again. And again. With each one of your kids. Until your quiver is empty. Just as God planned.

Laughter

…brings contentment.
…reveals partnership.
…defuses anger.
…turns strangers into friends.

Now, a few quick hints for ensuring a lifetime of laughs in your family…

Get a dog

Cubby, a mutt purchased for $30 from a shelter, was Randy's dog. Madison, the lovable, unflappable golden retriever, was Rae Anne's dog. Briggs, the speedy, entertaining silky terrier, is Rita's dog.

Here are some things I have learned from Cubby, Madison, and Briggs. They are a hassle when you go on vacation—whether you take them with, board them, or arrange for a dog sitter. They require vaccinations and occasional costly and emotional trips to the vet. They frighten mail carriers and nip neighbor boys. They will eat coins and mouse poison, leading to additional costly and emotional trips to the vet. They chew things. Your wife will worry about them. Goofing with them and laughing at them will become a natural connecting point for you and your children.

If you are intentional about it, having a dog can lead to conversations about responsibility, nutrition, loyalty, safety, sex, reproduction, breastfeeding, leaving home, boundaries, putting shoes away, and unconditional love.

When it comes time to put your beloved dog down, I recommend you give your son or daughter the option of waiting outside while the vet does her work. But I think I know what they'll do. Randy stayed with Cubby and a decade later Rae Anne stayed with Madison. I watched as those two wonderful creatures passed into eternity with their young masters stroking them gently and thanking them for being part of our family.

And how about cats, you ask? Pffft. Don't bother. The only thing cats can teach is how to be aloof and self-centered.

Take a miserable family vacation

One dad, one mom, five kids. One minivan. Driving from Chicago to Washington DC to experience our nation's capital. Our oldest, Alec, is heading into his senior year of high school. Rae Anne is four. The three middle children—Randy, Max, and Isaac—endure constantly changing levels of mutual love, laughter, and pounding.

The budget and schedule are both tight. The day we set aside to tour the White House, it's closed to the public. We're five minutes late for the tour of the FBI building, causing us to lose our place in line, which adds two hours to the wait. A lightning storm closes the Washington Monument as we're in the elevator. And it's possible that I started to pull out of a DC parking space with nine-year-old Isaac halfway out the side door of the minivan. Did I mention that the entire trip included 37 hours in a minivan?

The most memorable moment of the entire trip occurred when the other six members of my family were hustling to meet me at a predetermined location. Alec heroically gets his brothers ready to go. My wife wrestles our young and feisty daughter into a cute little outfit. The six of them maneuver over to, down in, on, off, and up from the Metro. Alec and Rita each held one of Rae Anne's hands. In the middle of a busy DC sidewalk, sweet Rae Anne stops in her tracks, yanks her hands out from the grasp of her mom and oldest brother, and fiercely asks the timely and astute question: "What's a vacation again?"

At the time it wasn't funny. But as you may imagine, the story has taken on a life of its own. Even now, when a family member schedules too many activities during a long weekend they'll stop in their tracks and do their best impression of four-year-old Rae Anne: "What's a vacation again?"

Even better, years later Alec discovered a postcard he had written to his girlfriend during that trip. Dripping with sarcasm, it read, "I'm having so much fun. I never want to come home."

I would say, "You had to be there." But hopefully you *have* been there. Or *will* be there. These kinds of non-life-threatening disasters result in classic family stories told again and again. You see, there's no way Rae Anne can remember that so-called vacation. She was only four. But she has heard that tale so many times that it has become part of her mental file cabinet of family memories.

It proves again that much of life is a matter of perspective. My family wouldn't trade the memory of those three days in our nation's capital for anything. If you had asked us in the middle of it, we might have had a different answer.

Shoot everyday video

I have schlepped around video cameras to hundreds of games, matches, concerts, and performances. You name it, I schlepped it. I recorded direct to VHS, VHS-C, MiniDV, and straight to flash memory. I first hoisted an early VHS Panasonic camcorder to my shoulder sometime when Alec was in grade school. The battery on that beast was about five times the size of my iPhone.

The irony is that very few feet of the existing analog or digital tape capture the personalities of my kids. Most of it is kind of boring. I shot wrestling matches so the boys could review their technique later that weekend. I shot panorama shots of lake cottages and Mount Rushmore to prove we were there. I shot birthday parties with lots of images of kids I don't even remember, so no one felt left out. Standing in the back of the gymnasium with a hundred other dads, I shot choir and band concerts because they were events on a calendar. And of course, there's nothing wrong with any of that.

But the video segments we much prefer to pull out and watch as a family today—and laugh and laugh and laugh—are simply the Payleitners doing everyday things. Such as Alec playing "Chopsticks" on the piano with one-year-old Rae Anne. The video of Isaac (whose name means "laughter," by the way) talking to his imaginary friend. All seven of us sitting in the floor in a small bedroom playing keep away with a rubber chicken. Four boys under ten in the same tub. Randy pouting on the stairs, banished there as a punishment. All much more entertaining than any reality TV show.

Got it? A videotaped game of middle school basketball might never be watched again, but your family playing cutthroat driveway basketball is priceless. So Dad, don't shoot video every day. But do shoot everyday video.

Best idea yet: tonight, pull out a tape from at least five years ago and see how the hairstyles, clothing, and voices have changed.

Be their coach for a season

This is a no-brainer for some dads. You live for this. But even if you're not athletically inclined, I recommend that every dad spend a season with a whistle, clipboard, and roster filled with ragtag kids who all wear the same color of T-shirt.

You don't have to be the head coach. Volunteer to assist. Or schedule practices. Or keep statistics. Or rake the field. (Just don't volunteer to do snacks. Real men don't organize snacks. That's what team moms are for.)

The benefits are many. You get to see your child in a new environment. You get to be close to the action, watching them grimace, grit their teeth, sweat, breathe, and stare down their opponent. You are forced to spend time with them. In the car. On the bench. Waiting for rain delays and late refs. Your young star (or nonstar) gets to see you at your best and your worst.

If your son or daughter continues on to a trophy-winning career complete with scholarships and pro contracts, you can take all the credit. Hey, you were there at the start, right? On the other hand, if they are just terrible and you are an even worse coach, cut your losses after one season. But have no regrets. You'll have something to laugh about together—especially when they find excellence and redemption in some nonsports arena.

Either way, hang that whistle on your tie rack and let it remind you of that championship season you spent as your kid's coach.

Make crazy memories

When you pull into our driveway at the end of the cul-de-sac, you might think it's just a driveway. You would be wrong. It's an arena, event center, workshop, and much more.

Our driveway has been the site of a pig roast, a sidewalk chalk art gallery, intense four-square contests, amateur auto-body repair, unicycle riding, tandem bike maintenance, science experiments including the old Mentos in the Diet Coke trick, home-run derbies, homecoming pep-rally practices, skateboard/bike skiing, slam-dunk contests, and dozens of games of stickball. One year, to celebrate their high-school graduation, we crafted an eight-foot-by-twelve-foot mosaic of

Isaac and his cousin Stephanie made entirely out of three-by-three Post-It notes and stuck it on our garage door.

Our backyard has seen even more amazing spectacles. The one I like to tell best is when I purchased the entire Wendy's Dollar Menu. Twice.

One summer evening Randy and Max were extolling the virtue, value, and tastiness of the Wendy's Dollar Menu.

Somehow speculation began regarding whether or not it was possible for one individual to consume one of everything—three burgers, one chicken sandwich, chicken nuggets, chili, fries, baked potato, salad, frosty, and beverage of choice—all in one sitting.

Somehow that idea became a contest pitting the 20-year-old against the 17-year-old in a battle of wills and stomach-stretching. Somehow Dad paid for the entire event.

The folks at Wendy's should be glad we didn't use their dining room. Instead the sacks of fast food were spread out on our picnic table while friends and family gathered for the unlikely competitive feast. Details are sketchy. I do remember it wasn't pretty. Years later, both boys claim some kind of victory. But the truth is, Randy and Max both wisely gave up with a few burgers still left in their wrappings.

It was probably the best $22 plus tax I spent that summer. The howls of laughter still echo through our backyard and family room.

Bragging rights remain unclaimed. But I'll claim victory for silly dads everywhere. When you hang out with (or near) your kids, wacky and wonderful ideas come up. You can squash them with a dose of common sense. Or you can surrender to the moment.

I submit that anytime you can enter their world with creativity and laughter, you have opened the door an inch further when it comes time for serious conversations later in life.

Laugh with your kids, Satan loses

Maybe one of the best reasons to laugh with your kids is because Satan hates happy families. His goal is make your home a place of door-slamming and despair. John 10:10 says, "The thief comes only to steal and kill and destroy; I have come that they may have life, and have it to the full."

If you're really courageous, you might even consider laughing at the devil himself. A thoughtful editorial in *Christianity Today* by Anderson M. Rearick III suggests we put Satan on notice that with Jesus on our side, he has no power over us.

> Should the forces of evil be mocked? Should Satan be laughed at? He most certainly should be. At the beginning of *The Screwtape Letters*, C. S. Lewis includes two telling quotations, the first from Martin Luther: "The best way to drive out the devil, if he will not yield to texts of Scripture, is to jeer and flout him, for he cannot bear scorn." The second comes from Thomas More: "The devil...the proud spirit cannot endure to be mocked." The one thing Satan cannot bear is to be a source of laughter. His pride is undermined by his own knowledge that his infernal rebellion against God is in reality an absurd farce.

As dads, we can further frustrate Satan by arming our children for spiritual battle. Our weapons are the fruit of the spirit—love, joy, peace, patience, kindness, goodness, faithfulness, gentleness, and self-control. Laughter is not on the list, but you can imagine it interwoven into each of those gifts. You can also imagine Satan in the corner grinding his teeth in frustration when a family sits around a dinner table, campfire, or family room sharing a story, memory, song, or laugh.

Humor is one of the most effective tools in your fathering toolbox. It often crops up when you least expect it. But dads can also be intentional about creating an atmosphere where laughter is propagated and cultivated. That could even mean telling knock-knock jokes, texting comic strips, buying tickets to a clean comedy event, or planning an elaborate practical joke. But always take care. As stated above, some humor such as sarcasm and coarse talk can easily go too far. Teasing or mocking also sets a dangerous precedent.

Sometimes dads get caught up in the moment, and we don't know when we're crossing the line from words that elevate to words that sting. The best humor for fathers might be the self-deprecating kind in which the laughter is directed back at you. Dad, I think you can take it. Especially if your kids are laughing right along with you.

Questions to Get Them Talking

1. **How many times per day do you laugh out loud?**

   Talking point: On some level, you don't want to turn laughter into a science. But you might certainly talk to your children about what makes them laugh. There are some videos, sitcom episodes, children's books, visual images, and phrases that literally make me laugh out loud. Especially when it comes to my kids. I should make a list and keep it handy. So should you!

2. **Do I ever embarrass you with your friends?**

   Talking point: Give your children permission to come to you—respectfully—when you've gone a little too far. Don't feel bad if your teenager has friends over to play a game or watch a movie and you're not invited. The kids are at your house and that's a good thing! On the other hand, you need to always feel comfortable entering their world and interacting for a few moments now and then. You'll be even more welcome if you bring a pizza with you.

3. **In the Disney Pixar movie *Monsters, Inc.*, laughter turned out to be more powerful than screams. Do you think that's true?**

   Talking point: It is possible to actually have a dialogue with a five-year-old. Whatever side they take, go ahead and plead the other side for a while. And then, no matter what arguments they present, tell them they made a good point.

4. **What's your favorite family memory?**

   Talking point: Laughter was probably part of any positive

family memory. You may not specifically remember something that triggered laughter. But the good feelings that wash through your memory were caused by the release of endorphins that most likely were produced by laughter.

5. **Did you know that you were a gift to me from God?**

Talking point: Open to Psalm 127 and point out the verse, "Children are a gift from the LORD; they are a reward from him." Then say, "Boy, if you knuckleheads are my reward, I hate to think what God's punishment might be!"

Conversations to Pursue

- *Want to give your high schooler a good laugh?* Pull out your yearbooks. Make special note of hairstyles, uniforms, and any autographs and memories scribbled in the margins.

- *Read Ecclesiastes 3 with your kids.* It includes "a time to tear down and a time to build, a time to weep and a time to laugh, a time to mourn and a time to dance…" Talk about the seasons of life. And the cycles that happen even within a day or week. When your kids are hurting, it helps to know that joy will return.

- *If your dad was the strong, silent type,* you may be tempted to lament a lack of hugs and laughter in your boyhood home. Instead, I recommend you cut him some slack. As long as he wasn't oppressive, be grateful for the provision, protection, and strength of character he brought to the family. Tell your kids about your dad. And ask if there are ways you can be a better father.

- *Accidents happen.* Kids spill their milk. They know they messed up. They're already sorry. Yelling will only make it worse. When the milk glass tumbles, your best course of action is to throw napkins at the spill, give a chuckle, and say, "That's a pretty big puddle for such a little glass. No problem."

- *Three classic knock-knock jokes:*

    Knock-knock.
    Who's there?
    Lettuce.
    Lettuce who?
    Lettuce in, it's cold out here.

    Knock-knock.
    Who's there?
    Wooden shoe.
    Wooden shoe who?
    Wooden shoe like to know?

    Knock-knock.
    Who's there?
    Dwayne.
    Dwayne who?
    Dwayne the bathtub, I'm dwowning.

On Love, Sex, and Marriage

"Where does the family start? It starts with a young man falling in love with a girl—no superior alternative has yet been found.

Winston Churchill

"There is no more lovely, friendly, and charming relationship, communion, or company than a good marriage."

Martin Luther

Of all the conversations described in this book, the conversation on sex might be the most daunting for dads.

It might help to approach the topic just like all the others. Specifically: Remind yourself that you want what's best for your kids. Consider the practical, moral, and spiritual imperatives of the topic. Recognize that as young people mature, they are going to face some crossroads and decisions. Welcome their questions and concerns. And engage them on their level with optimism and a dash of humor. Try to remain nonthreatening, nonjudgmental, and nonpanicky.

I hope it's okay that we're covering romantic love, sex, and marriage in one chapter. There are volumes and entire libraries devoted to each of these topics. But in God's plan, I believe they weave a single tapestry. If you think about it for ten seconds, you'll find yourself agreeing that all three are interdependent. As a matter of fact, all three *must* go together. Otherwise, something is missing. If we can get our growing children to understand the beauty in that design, we've done them a great service.

Model a great marriage

Four of my favorite people in the world are named Payleitner. And they got that name in the last few years. Rachel, Lindsay, Megan, and Kaitlin married my sons. And I couldn't be more delighted.

It's very easy for me to envision those four couples staying committed to each other for a lifetime. Sure, they're young. And their marriages will go through seasons of disagreement and discouragement. But they have a few things in their favor that will help them survive any storms to find deeper love, romance, and commitment on the other side.

First, they've got statistics in their favor. My parents were married 60 years. Rita and I have been married (yikes!) more than 35 years. A recent study was commissioned to determine if genetics was a factor in predicting divorce. Instead, researchers were surprised to discover that "children of divorced parents are roughly twice as likely to see their own marriage end in divorce."[2] Rita and I are taking no credit—well, maybe a little—but it appears our long marriage literally increases the chances that my kids will have long marriages. They will merely be continuing the precedent that began with my parents…and my parents' parents. (These are not absolutes, of course, so please don't take anything for granted.)

Second, God has been invited into their marriage unions. And his undeniable desire is to keep families together. As has been said, "God was at your wedding; now invite him to your marriage." An illustration I saw years ago helped me tremendously to visualize this idea. Imagine a triangle with God at the top and a husband and wife at the two bottom corners. At the base of the triangle, they are miles apart. But the closer the man and woman get to God, the closer they are to each other. Can you picture it? Draw it out for your kids. That's a conversation starter right there.

Then, back it up with more research. A 2008 study issued by the

Center for Marriage and Families concluded that couples 18 to 55 who attend church services several times a month report happier marriages than those who rarely or never attend church.[3]

Even more compelling—and maybe surprising to you—is a study in the *Journal for the Scientific Study of Religion* that disproves a rumor that has been circulating for years. You have probably heard the conventional wisdom that the divorce rate is the same for Christians and nonbelievers. Well, that's just not true. It turns out marriages in which both husband and wife attend church frequently are 2.4 times *less likely* to end in divorce than marriages in which neither spouse attends religious services.[4]

Ready to expand on this point? Consider this circular process: strengthening your commitment to your spouse gets you closer to God, which strengthens your commitment to your spouse. See if you can sneak that into a conversation with a teenager.

Kiss your wife in the kitchen

You need to be able to tell your kids that you love their mom. You want to be able to say to them, "I love being married. Someday if you get married, I pray that you'll love your wife (or husband) as much as I love your mom."

That kind of bold statement needs to be backed up with action. That's why I recommend regularly making out with your wife right in the busiest room in the house. It achieves three worthy objectives. It tells your bride you love her. It tells your kids you love their mom. It demonstrates to your kids that passion can happen in a committed, lifelong marriage relationship.

Most of the kisses your kids see on television or in movies are couples who are not married. (At least to each other.) Hollywood seems to think that once a couple is married, sex becomes less than interesting. After the wedding, the romance is gone, so to speak. Well, I disagree. And so does God:

Enjoy life with your wife, whom you love (Ecclesiastes 9:9).

May you rejoice in the wife of your youth…may her breasts satisfy you always, may you ever be intoxicated by her love (Proverbs 5:18-19).

So kiss your bride in the kitchen. The goal is for your fourth-grader to go "Ewwww!" or your teenager to wisecrack, "Get a room!" That's a sure signal you're doing it right.

Be an awesome husband

You're being watched. Your son is learning how to act. And your daughter is taking notes to figure out what she wants in a husband. Listen carefully, because in one paragraph I'm going to save you $12.99 and summarize my book *52 Things Wives Need from Their Husbands.* Ready?

Cherish her. Encourage her dreams. Honor her desires. Don't keep score about who did what last to whom. Don't say stuff you already know will tick her off. Really listen. Be the first to apologize. Be the spiritual leader in your home. Surprise her with flowers. Buy sparkly gifts. Choose to only have eyes for her. Flee pornography. Remove all competition. Believe your bride is the most beautiful woman in the world. Control your anger. Be patient in the bedroom. Stay married.

Maybe most important, anticipate the seasons of marriage. You will make mistakes. She will disappoint you. Kids will exhaust both of you. Kids will delight both of you. Friends will come and go. Jobs will be lost. Cash may be tight. Illness will come. And small miracles will unfold at just the right time. Let all of life—the good and bad—bring the two of you closer together. Through it all, trust love. You know 1 Corinthians 13. Someone probably read it or sang it at your wedding. It's the "love chapter" of the Bible that begins and ends, "Love is patient, love is kind…it always protects, always trusts, always hopes, always perseveres. Love never fails."

So trust love. Persevere. Being an awesome husband is a true gift to your growing son or daughter. Even better, it increases the chance of you loving and living with an awesome wife.

Make sure your kids respect their mom

I have a fantastic wife. If it weren't for Rita, I would likely be living in a van down by the river. She's easy to love and has earned my respect and admiration.

Honestly, I don't know what it's like to be in long-term conflict with my wife. I don't know what it's like to be antagonistic or adversarial. I don't know what it's like to be separated or divorced, wondering why I'm not living happily ever after, scraping up child support, and agonizing over my inability to see my kids. If that describes your life, then my heart aches for you and your entire family.

Dad, if you've been through a divorce, then you have some extra work to do. At some point, you may want to acknowledge your share of the responsibility for past mistakes. Make extra effort to be respectful of your children's mom. Treat her with dignity. Refrain from shouting, blaming, or name-calling. Respond to her requests, keep the lines of communication open, and work things out in a way that is as fair as possible to all parties involved.

Respect, common courtesy, and communication are not just priorities for divorced, separated, or never-married dads. That's the bare minimum for any and all husbands.

Talk about God's plan for marriage

This book is not a marriage manual. But for the sake of your kids, you want to portray marriage—one man, one woman, in a lifetime commitment—to be a worthy goal. Talk naturally about God's plan for marriage. And why it works. Explain that marriage is not a business relationship, legal contract, or a stage of life that happens for convenience or by accident. The second chapter in the Bible spells it out: "A man leaves his father and mother and is united to his wife, and they become one flesh" (Genesis 2:24).

What does it mean to "become one flesh"? Even if they don't ask that question, go ahead and answer it. Becoming one flesh is what happens when you say, "I do," on your wedding day. It also happens in the marriage bed—emotionally, spiritually, and physically. A neurochemical reaction of dopamine and oxytocin floods the brain to bond men and women having sex. Becoming one flesh also defines the journey of a husband and wife traveling through life together. They carry each other in good times and not-so-good times. They celebrate and console. They love each other unconditionally. They give and receive. All of the above connections are designed by the Creator.

Some couples describe their marriage as 50/50. Their motivation for serving each other is, "You had your turn, now it's my turn." Or "If I do this for her, she will do something else for me." That might work for a while, but the relationship is reduced to a series of transactions. That flawed marital logic suggests if your spouse can't or won't do their part, then you owe them nothing. That's not a marriage, that's two people doing business. I think God had a better idea. As one flesh, you do something because it elevates and serves *both of you*. Your motivation is "If I do this for her, it brings me joy as well." That's not 50/50. That's 100/100.

No matter what your relationship is with your children's mother, think this idea through—and own it. When the topic of marriage comes up, express optimism to your kids with sincerity and hope for their future.

Make sure they know how the plumbing works

In our town, in fifth grade, all the public school students get a basic lesson in how babies are made.

I believe the timing is motivated by the desire that no young ladies are surprised and panicked by their first menstrual period. That's a worthy goal. (And a topic dads surely don't want to think about.) Fifth-grade boys, of course, are all over the place when it comes to what they know, don't know, or think they know. Their surprise will come a few years later when about four out of five boys experience nocturnal emissions (a.k.a. "wet dreams," which is something dads *do* need to mention.)

To clarify what you're dealing with, by fifth grade just about every boy and girl has already seen tantalizing onscreen images of partially naked bodies lying on top of other partially naked bodies. Even if you fiercely monitor every movie and television show, sexualized content will show up in movie trailers, commercials, and PG comedies. Not to mention actual graphic pornography that is always a few clicks away on screens—large and small.

As sophisticated as they think they are, it's almost amusing how little kids really know. Most are too embarrassed to bring it up, even though they're quite curious. Dad, I recommend you use that curiosity to your advantage. *Months before* your school presents their "sex-ed curriculum," find the right time and the right place to bring up the subject with your child.

Frankly, I recommend dads talk to sons and moms talk to daughters. I'm well aware that a small, but significant, percentage of dads are raising young girls by themselves. And those daughters are rapidly approaching womanhood. If that describes you, then begin looking now for the right aunt, grandmother, close friend who happens to be a nurse or doctor, or mom of one of your daughter's friends to help with this conversation. Your daughter will appreciate your sensitivity and follow-through.

My four conversations with my four sons will not be documented here. But I will recommend that fathers initiate that first breakthrough conversation with a son while driving to an out-of-town sporting event—a professional game or a game in which your son is participating. It's a pretty solid strategy. You have a captive audience, the two of you can avoid eye contact, long periods of silence are perfectly acceptable, and the conversation can end naturally when you pull up to the field.

How long will this conversation take? Somewhere between seven minutes and two hours. Don't expect a lot of questions. Instead, go ahead and fill in most of the blanks yourself. If it turns into mostly a monologue, that's okay. But see if you can sprinkle in some easy-to-answer questions along the way. I would never tell you exactly what to say, but some of your riffs might go something like this:

"I believe that this coming school year, you and your classmates are going

to spend a few weeks talking about where babies come from. You probably know a lot of this stuff already. But I'm thinking this is something you
and I need to be able to talk about. Have you heard anything about that
at school?"

"Umm. Not really. Maybe a little."

"We used to call it 'sex education.' They probably have some silly name
for it now. I'm not sure exactly what the school is going to cover, but I
wanted you to hear it from me first. I'm just going to start with the basics
and go from there. And you can ask any question at any time, okay?"

[SILENCE.]

"Here goes. First, this is all designed by God. And is part of his plan.
[CHUCKLE] I guess even a dad talking to his son about sex and pregnancy
is part of God's plan too. It may get a little embarrassing. For you and for
me. But it's all good. Any questions?"

"We're going to do this now?"

"Yup. I promise to be as efficient as possible. Let's see. Ummm. Boys and
girls are different. Thank goodness. Here are the basics: Only girls can get
pregnant. Boys have penises. Girls have vaginas. It takes an egg from the
woman and sperm from the man to make a baby. One sperm fertilizes one
egg inside the mom and that becomes an embryo. When that happens, that
embryo has the complete DNA that decides just about everything about
that baby. If it's a boy or girl. What color eyes and hair. Health factors.
Fingerprints. It takes nine months to fully grow in the mom's tummy—the
mom's uterus. You knew all that, right?"

"Pretty much."

"Nine months is best. You were actually two weeks early. Which was
not a problem. Babies average six or seven pounds. You were five pounds,
ten ounces…I think. You were perfect. Still are. Anyway. Nine months is
best. Babies can be born premature, even at six months—even just two
pounds—and still make it. But they spend a lot of time in the hospital. Are
you with me?"

"Sure."

"So how does that sperm get to the egg? It's called sexual intercourse…"

And that's as far as I'm going to go in my pretend conversation. I hope you get the idea and I also hope you can muster the courage, wisdom, and winsome attitude to finish the talk.

To help you prepare, here are a few more short non-preachy sermons you may want to deliver proactively or in response to a question.

"Twins happen when two eggs are fertilized at the same time. Usually that's two sperms swimming up to and fertilizing two eggs creating two separate embryos. Identical twins happen when an embryo splits soon after conception into two embryos that are genetically the same."

"There are all kinds of slang terms for body parts and for intercourse. You can ask me about any of them at any time. But 'having sex' is sometimes called 'making love' or 'doing it' or 'going all the way.' You've heard the 'f-word.' That's another one. Some of the terms get nasty. Which is a shame because as God designed it, in marriage, sex is really a great gift shared between a husband and wife. But you probably don't want to think about that, right?"

"The word 'adultery' is when someone who is married has sex with someone they're not married to. That explains the seventh commandment, 'You shall not commit adultery'" (Exodus 20:14).

"An orgasm is when semen is released from the man and received by the woman. It's a good feeling for both the husband and wife. God designed it that way to help bond a man and woman for life. God wants married men and women to have sex to celebrate their love and because babies are good things. God wanted Adam and Eve to make babies. In the very first chapter of the Bible, it says, 'God blessed them and said to them, "Be fruitful and increase in number; fill the earth and subdue it."'"

"AIDS is 'acquired immune deficiency syndrome.' It's one of dozens of different STIs, which stands for 'sexually transmitted infections.' Others are syphilis, gonorrhea, HPV, herpes, genital warts, and other diseases that are hard to pronounce. HIV is the virus that leads to AIDS. When I was a kid, AIDS was just discovered. It was one of the top news stories of the 1980s. There was no cure and thousands of homosexual men died from AIDS. Lots of controversy. AIDS soon spread to the heterosexual community. There's still no cure, but people who have HIV can take drugs to slow the virus from multiplying."

"*Ready for some statistics? There are more than 19 million new cases of STIs in the U.S. every year. Half of the sexually active people under 25 have an STI. That means, on a college campus, about half the people walking around have an infection in their private parts and will probably have it for the rest of their lives.*"

"*Good news. There is a way to stop sexually transmitted infections 100 percent. How do you think that is? Here's a hint: If you only have sex with one person and neither of you have ever had sex before, then you are virtually 100 percent safe. By the way, that's God's plan.*"

"*I'm not sure what will be covered in your fifth-grade sex class. Talking about STIs might be too scary. And it should be scary! Symptoms are rashes, yeast infections, fever, burning sensation when you urinate, warts. One of the scariest things is that there may be no symptoms for a while and people just pass STIs on from one sexual partner to the next. All of which reminds me of one of my favorite Bible verses, 'Flee from sexual immorality' (1 Corinthians 6:18). Sounds like a pretty good plan, doesn't it?*"

"*Freshman year of high school, health classes may cover how to prevent pregnancy and STIs. Even if they don't, you'll probably hear about condoms. A condom is a latex sleeve—almost like a balloon—that the man slides over his penis before sex to catch the semen. Two things about condoms. They don't always work to prevent pregnancy—there's a 15 percent failure rate.[5] And they can't prevent all STIs.*"

The goal is to share facts, your personal values, and biblical truth all at the same time. The culture sometimes tries to separate this stuff into convenient boxes, but it's all interconnected: romantic love/sex/marriage/God's design/common sense/logic/science/biblical application.

It's not surprising that the way in which parents handle "the sex talk" has a significant impact on whether or not young people grow up to trust God or turn their back on him. By the way, "the sex talk" is not a single event. It's a progressive father-child interaction that begins when you sing that first lullaby and continues when they begin to notice the difference between boys and girls. By the time you get to the more complicated stuff, the foundation should already be in place.

As with any conversation you have with your kids, don't make stuff up. If they ask about something you don't know, promise you'll do some research and get back to them. And then follow through on that promise.

With boys, don't expect a lot of follow-up questions. I speak from experience. One summer afternoon, I switched off the TV after another late-inning loss by our beloved Chicago Cubs and invited one of my sons to run an errand. It was time for "the talk." After a not-too-painful fifteen-minute conversation during which I did most of the talking, I asked if he had any questions. After a long pause, he said, "Why didn't Dernier tag up and try to score in the eighth inning?" That was my son's way of saying that he understood what I was saying, needed some time to process the information, and would really like to change the subject. Of course, I was relieved. Mostly because I knew the answer to his critical question. It was either bad coaching or bad base-running.

Why wait?

I had the privilege of producing *Josh McDowell Radio* for 14 years. At the time, Josh was focusing quite a bit of energy on the "Why Wait?" campaign, which meant we recorded several broadcasts on sexual purity, abstinence, and the relationships between parents and teenagers. As a dad with five kids, I learned right along with our radio audience.

We did entire shows on topics like STIs, how to say no to sexual pressure, dating strategies, and the flaws in comprehensive sexual education. But I always thought the most effective broadcasts helped answer the question upon which the entire campaign was built: "Why should a young person wait until they're married to have sex?"

Let's consider some possible strategies:

- Scare tactics built around STIs might work for some. But even when presented with clear facts, teenagers see themselves as indestructible.

- "Because God says so" is a hard sell to teenagers who already have lots of questions about God.

- Parents sometimes use the old standard condemnation of sex as dirty or evil, but that's totally inaccurate. And just introducing that idea is likely damaging to your child's future marriage relationship.

- Ominously saying, "You can only give away your virginity one time," might not work anymore because "everyone else is doing it." To a high schooler, being a virgin seems to have lost its value and may even be a term of ridicule.

- Getting pregnant has also lost much of its fear factor. Teenagers have easy access to birth control, abortion is considered a viable option, and lots of teenagers are keeping their babies and even getting federal aid. Besides, in the heat of the moment, they don't think it can happen to them.

- Sex while you're dating might convince you to marry the wrong person. You mistake sex for love. In a marriage, sex creates a physical and emotional bond. Outside of marriage that can be very confusing. The problem is that when young people hear that argument, they think you're trashing their boyfriend or girlfriend.

- You could say, "Having premarital sex will fill you with guilt and remorse." However, that's not what they're hearing from their friends or seeing in the media.

So…why wait? It's a legitimate question and you need to have an answer that penetrates the head, heart, and soul of your child.

First, don't throw out any of the above ideas. They all still make a valid point. STIs are scary. God does make it clear—sex outside of marriage is a sin. Saving yourself for marriage is an empowering choice. A pregnant, unmarried teen is most definitely in crisis. Sex outside of marriage *does* cause emotional chaos. And there is a negative emotional downside to sex when there's no lifetime commitment. But there's more.

Here's where I think the relationship you've built with your child will make all the difference. You've demonstrated many times that you want what's best for them. You love them unconditionally. You've talked about the many gifts God has given to them. As part of God's creation, they've been given the gift of life, the beauty of nature, and the love of family and friends. As individuals, you've pointed out their unique gifts and talents. How there is a wonderful plan for their life. You've proven they are loved by you and by God. You've prayed *for* them and *with* them. You've even prayed for the health and well-being of their future spouse—even though the identity of that individual might be a complete mystery. You've provided for their needs. You've laughed with them and cried with them.

You're their dad. But that alone is not enough. You've taken the time and earned the right to speak truth into their life. And so just say it.

"Sex is more than physical. You know that. And the biology of sex is something you can find online or in textbooks. Just as important—actually more important—is the goal of accepting this wonderful gift from God and opening it at the right time with the right person. Part of it is to protect you. Saving yourself until after your wedding will protect you from guilt, disease, pregnancy, comparisons with other partners, and heartbreak.

"But the reason to wait is so much more than that. God has given you this beautiful expression of love to share one day with your husband/your wife. You can only open it once. And the idea of giving yourself only to each other—forsaking all others—discovering together what love really means as husband and wife is my prayer for you. That's why the Bible teaches, 'Marriage should be honored by all, and the marriage bed kept pure' (Hebrews 13:4). It's not just to protect you, it's to provide the kind of love that far too many couples never experience. But some day you can."

Offer your help

Well before they begin dating, the goal is threefold:

1. Get them to understand and acknowledge the value of waiting.

2. Get them to make a decision to wait.

3. Get their permission to help them along the way.

Dad, these aren't boxes you can check off yourself. They are decisions your son or daughter needs to make for themselves. You may want to think of this list as three thresholds that need to be crossed over the course of several conversations. One, then two, then three.

Also, anticipate that a teenager who has already enjoyed a goodnight kiss on the front porch will not readily agree to such matters. They might, but it's much easier to get their attention and agreement before the lustful attraction of young love kicks in.

Once you do have their permission to offer help, then by all means take full advantage. Set curfews. Meet their boyfriends and girlfriends. And their parents. Set dating standards. Encourage group dating. Make house rules such as not being behind a closed bedroom door or in the house alone together. And no texting after 11 p.m.

Don't drive them crazy with constant grilling and a barrage of questions after each date, but keep your promise. You did promise to help them keep their commitment to wait.

And, good dads keep their promises.

The love paradox

It may or may not come up. And you may or may not want to bring it up. But every young man or woman swept up in the romance of the century will ask themselves, "Is this love?"

The short answer is, "Love is authentic when it's unconditional." That means you love someone for who they are, no matter what, even if they disappoint you, and even if you go through a season when you lose all the emotional (gooshy) feelings of love.

Dad, if and when your teenager announces they're "in love," it's a good idea not to dismiss, mock, or deny that feeling. Because it's very real. So just go with it. Say as few words as possible. The reply, "Ah, that's wonderful," comes to mind. Conversely, if your 16-year-old announces she's getting married next week, then launch into a longer conversation. Much longer.

Love itself is a good thing. Don't ever try to crush it. It may be hard to take your child seriously, but don't talk down to them. Don't call them immature or laugh at their silly "puppy love." Instead talk about seasons of love. Talk about how it's tempting for someone their age to surrender a piece of their heart to someone. That's natural. Tell them, "You need to go slow. Your heart—your love and devotion—are precious commodities. Anything you give away might be gone forever. You want your heart intact when the time comes for your forever commitment." Dating or courting means entering unpredictable territory. They are going to discover new things about the other person—and themselves. It takes time. There will be highs and lows. Don't skip too fast through the seasons.

We referred to 1 Corinthians 13 earlier in this chapter as a reminder to trust love. It also can be used as a convenient checklist to test love. Have your daughter insert her boyfriend's name into the Scripture text: "Ben is patient, Ben is kind. Ben does not envy. He does not boast. He is not proud. Ben does not dishonor others, he is not self-seeking. Ben is not easily angered, he keeps no record of wrongs. Ben does not delight in evil but rejoices with the truth. Ben always protects, always trusts, always hopes, always perseveres. Ben never fails." How does the young suitor, Ben, stack up?

As impossible as that list sounds, it does help set worthy goals and suggest some limits and expectations your daughter should establish in her relationship with Ben and all future relationships.

Tell your teenager that their current season of love should have limits. Only love within a marriage has no limits. Which brings us back to a slightly longer answer for the original question, "Is this love?"

Here goes. "Love is authentic when you no longer have to do anything to get love in return. And you no longer feel *required* to do anything to get love in return. And at the same time, your beloved no longer has to do anything to be loved by you. And, your beloved no longer feels *required* to do anything to be loved by you."

That's unconditional love. No action is required. No kissing. No sex. No financial requirements. No flowers, no candy. No anniversaries to remember. No lists to check. It's love without conditions. Now before you or your starry-eyed teenager push back with all kinds of obvious arguments, allow me to remind you of the love paradox.

Unconditional love overflows into unselfish action. So love is a verb. Love does lead to action. Wonderful, generous, thoughtful actions. Suddenly, the love paradox is not really that confusing after all.

Questions to Get Them Talking

1. **Do you want to get married someday?**

   Talking point: With your little girl, talk about walking her down the aisle someday. With your young son, talk about finding the right bride to match his gifts and make him an even better man. Help each kid dream about building a home and family. And then make sure you earn the right to stay involved in their lives.

2. **I think dating may have changed since I was your age. Do girls ask boys out? Who pays for dates? Do boys still have to meet the girl's father?**

   Talking point: Allow your children to be the experts on today's dating scene. That will clue you in on what to expect as they move into serious dating. Be ready to push back if they say something that doesn't meet your standards.

3. **Newspaper advice columnists have a standard answer for the question, "How do I know if I'm in love?" They say, "If you have to ask, you're not." What do you think of that answer?**

   Talking point: There may be some truth to it. But it's probably a cop-out. The problem is, there are too many other emotions and physical sensations that can be mistaken for love. That includes being cared for, listened to, or respected. Patients fall in love with nurses. Students have a crush on a favorite teacher. Sexual arousal should never be mistaken for love, but it often is.

4. **How many girls at your high school are pregnant?**

   Talking point: There's a danger with assuming teenagers are sexually active. It's almost as if you're suggesting that premarital sex is unavoidable, so kids might as well just go for it. Still, depending on the size of their high school, you can easily assume that girls are getting pregnant, having abortions, and keeping their babies.

5. **When kids head off to college, I don't know what's scarier: STIs or "friends with benefits." What do you think?**

    Talking point: Asking this question of your high-school freshman would blow their mind. But being able to have adult conversations with your older teenagers about real-life topics is the goal. As part of a longer dialogue, you should be able to confirm that condoms might prevent some—but not all—sexually transmitted infections. They're effective in stopping pregnancy only about 85% of the time. Equally—or perhaps more—damaging is having multiple sex partners with no commitment. Casual promiscuity will crush the heart of a young adult. It sacrifices and steals the joy and intimacy from their future marriage. The takeaway from these conversations is that God's plan offers guarantees and absolutes. What the world offers is not even close to satisfying.

Conversations to Pursue

- *Talk about how and why God's plan is a pretty good one.* First, get married. Then have sex. Then have babies. Stay married. Raise kids together. There are lots of benefits across the board.

- *It's been said, "Men give love to get sex. And women give sex to get love."* With older teens, that quote could lead to an interesting conversation. It speaks to the physical urges of men and the emotional needs of women.

- *Here's an idea for dads and sons who share a love of sports.* Order *Sports Illustrated.* You can get a subscription without the annual swimsuit edition, but I recommend you let that issue come into your home. When it arrives, quietly walk it out to the trash can. Your son will know it's out; it's on all the news-stands and the release gets lot of media attention. He'll even-tually ask, "Hey, Dad, where's this week's *Sports Illustrated*?" That's when you say, "Oh, I tossed it. It was the Swimsuit Edi-tion. You don't need to see that. And frankly, I don't either. Does that make sense?" That could actually lead to a nice father-son conversation about how men need to respect women for who they are, not how they look.

- *You have to feel sorry for couples who don't understand the spir-itual side of sexual intimacy.* They're missing out. Like every-thing else, sex is a gift from God to be opened at just the right time. Make sure your kids know that.

- *If a spouse is tragically injured in a car accident* and left with no use of their arms or legs, can't speak, and has limited brain capacity, can they still love? Can they still be loved? Married couples need to have that kind of unconditional love.

- *How is God's plan for sex and marriage good for the culture?* Less crime (85 percent of the youth in prison grew up with-out a father). Less drug abuse (75 percent of teenagers in drug rehab come from fatherless homes). Less divorce. Girls who have had sex in their teens are about twice as likely to get divorced later on.[6]

On Decision Making

*"The greatest pleasure in life is doing
what people say you cannot do."*

Walter Bagehot

*"Suppose one of you wants to build a tower. Won't
you first sit down and estimate the cost to see
if you have enough money to complete it?"*

Luke 14:28

True story. My oldest son, Alec, was reading when he was in kindergarten. Real books with real chapters. Really. That following summer we signed him up for soccer. It was the first time any of my children were ever in an organized sport. At the time, I knew nothing about soccer. (Still don't, really.) But every kid in town seemed to be wearing a brightly colored Tri-Cities Soccer T-shirt, so we scraped together our $40 fee and plunged into the world of organized sports.

Since we were both soccer newbies, I thought my young son and I could bond over the discovery process. I took the logical step of checking a book out of the library titled something like *Beginning Soccer*. Alec and I took turns reading about forwards and sweepers. Dribbling and passing. Offsides and red cards. And, of course, using your hands only when you're the goalie or throwing the ball in. It was nice having a practical application for our bedtime reading ritual. Alec was looking forward to putting his new knowledge to work.

Well, if you've ever been to a soccer game played by five-year-olds, you know that it is nothing at all like any game described in a book about soccer. Before that first game, the coaches have to walk onto the field and literally show players where to stand. But as soon as the ref blows the first whistle there are no forwards, sweepers, and wingbacks. There is no dribbling or passing. There are no penalties. And sometimes players do use their hands. Games with young first-time players can best be described as ants on a sugar cube. Every kid on the field is doing the same thing—getting as close to the ball as possible and just kicking it. Where it goes doesn't matter.

During Alec's first game, there were actually two players who were not swarming the soccer ball. One boy in red shorts raced around the field as if he was being attacked by killer bees. And then there was Alec. The coach had sent him out to start the game as a midfielder. After he jogged to that spot on his own, the whistle blew and my brilliant, healthy, capable son literally never moved. Not a single step. He was petrified because he had too much information. He knew there was a strategy to the game. But the gaggle of players caroming around the field made no sense at all.

Rita and I watched helplessly, hoping our son's natural love of sports would kick in. I remember cheering, "Get the ball, Alec," and "Go after it." After five long minutes, mercifully the ref whistled for substitutions. That's when the situation went from bad to worse. Our coach looked at his clipboard and called out the subs he had predetermined before the game. We were dumbfounded when he didn't call Alec off the field. Before we realized it, play resumed and our son still hadn't left his original starting spot. I'll never forget what happened a minute later. Alec looked my way and called out, "Dad. Dad. I don't know what to do."

If you can imagine the scenario, you know that I wanted to stop play and run on the field to rescue him. That might have been the right choice. But this was my first experience ever as a dad on the sidelines and I felt just as helpless as my son.

When he finally did come off the field, I got down on one knee and we watched the game together. I pointed to one of the better players who seemed to have some basic skills and said, "Alec, you can do that. I know you can." That did not help his confidence. And then I changed tactics. I pointed to the young man in red shorts running around haphazardly with no apparent interest in the game or the ball. We watched for a bit and then I said, "Alec, can you at least do that?" That got a smile out of him. He went back in at the next substitution and played a solid second half, and even went on to enjoy a few more seasons of competitive soccer.

Still, more than 25 years later, I can remember his helpless voice, "Dad. Dad. I don't know what to do."

Looking back, there were no bad decisions made that day. As difficult as the situation was, there was no bad guy. No evil intent. Even the coach who had a chance to shorten the agony can't really be faulted. It was also his first game of the year and he had a dozen other players to corral. Really the greatest lesson is that whether we hear it or not, our children are often saying or thinking that same accurate and articulate phrase I heard coming from the field. My son didn't know what to do and he was counting on his dad for help.

A decision-making overview

Every human makes thousands, maybe millions, of decisions a day. Some we think long and hard about. Some we just do. Whether to take a sip of coffee before or after we bite our raspberry scone is a decision. Moving your family to do mission work in Czech Republic is a decision. Most decisions fall somewhere in between.

As a dad, you need to model good decision-making skills. Let's hit the nail on the head right away with five biblical absolutes you have readily available to make good decisions.

- *Pray.* "If any of you lacks wisdom, you should ask God, who gives generously to all without finding fault, and it will be given to you" (James 1:5).
- *Pursue God's will, not your own.* "There is a way which seems right to a man, but its end is the way of death" (Proverbs 14:12 NASB).

- *Turn to Scripture.* "Your word is a lamp for my feet, a light on my path" (Psalm 119:105).

- *Seek wise counsel.* "Plans fail for lack of counsel, but with many advisers they succeed" (Proverbs 15:22).

- *Trust God.* "Trust in the LORD with all your heart and lean not on your own understanding; in all your ways submit to him, and he will make your paths straight" (Proverbs 3:5-6).

Read that list again. Take it to heart. None of those admonitions should surprise you. Bookmark this page and open it anytime you or your children need to make a decision. Five steps. Got 'em?

This chapter could end there, but let's kick around a few more ideas that may come in handy as you push and pull your kids around the decision-making paths of life.

Do what's right in front of you

This would have been a good concept for five-year-old Alec to know that day on the soccer field. During those ten minutes he stood on the field, the ball traveled within a few feet of him several times. One good kick and he would have become part of the flow of the game.

But the concept of tackling the task right in front of you goes well beyond sports. How often do we find ourselves bored, confused, anxious, lacking confidence, lacking full funding, lacking the right tools, afraid of making a mistake, feeling like some task is undignified, feeling like the task is not worth the effort, or waiting for an engraved invitation? That happens quite often, right?

Not always, but a powerful principle is "just start." My agent Dan Balow used to say, "You can only steer a semitruck when it's moving." When your third-grader is stuck on his assignment to build a castle, you can help by finding the right piece of plywood for a base, but he needs to put up the first wall. After your freshman has stared at the blank screen for 20 minutes not knowing how to start her short story, tell her to type something, anything. Even if she just writes, "It was the best of times, it was the worst of times," that may flush away any writer's block. Later, remind her to rewrite or edit out the first sentence so she isn't accused of plagiarism.

The old Nike slogan, "Just do it," applies here quite nicely. Even better is the great Old Testament verse that instructs, "Whatever your hand finds to do, do it with all your might" (Ecclesiastes 9:10).

Are you modeling that for your children? Do they see you as a man of action? Or a man of excuses? Ask yourself if there are responsibilities and opportunities right in front of you. A hedge that needs trimming? A windowpane that needs replacing? A city council seat that needs some new blood? A mountain that needs climbing? A tree in your backyard that has the perfect branch configuration to support a tree house?

Sometimes the decision of *what to do* is easy. Do what's right in front of you.

Do the duty of the moment

Ah, but what's the difference between a "duty" and a "distraction"?

Sometimes the overgrown hedge needs to wait. Just because the mountain is there, doesn't mean you need to climb it today. And that tree house is not a one-day project.

Years ago, a dear pastor friend taught me a phrase that has driven much of my best efforts. Sometimes you just need to surrender to "the duty of the moment."

Work deadlines, organizing file cabinets, and balancing the checkbook are duties. Important ones. But they would rarely be described as a "duty of the moment." Maybe some examples would help:

- Your neighbor needs a lift to the mechanic.
- A recently downsized co-worker needs someone to look over his résumé.
- A new friend e-mails you, wanting directions to your church.
- Your wife gets word her best friend is going to need radiation therapy.

- Your son needs to show you his sketches of a new superhero.
- Your daughter needs one more guest at a tea party.

Actually these are easy decisions. Because love is the driving force behind each and every "duty of the moment." Sorry, work deadlines, demanding bosses, and bank accounts. You might have to wait an extra half hour while a man of integrity comforts his wife, does a favor for another human in need, or makes a connection with a child.

Is your son or daughter a procrastinator? You may think that clueing them in on "the duty of the moment" is a terrible idea. That you're just giving them another excuse to not do their homework, chores, and so on. Actually, the opposite is true. In your conversation with your child, define "the duty of the moment" as a short, worthwhile distraction. That definition opens the door to talk about how easy and dangerous it is to come up with excuses that take them away from their responsibilities.

When it comes to keeping your kids on task, you need to be able to say, "Hey, kiddo. It looks like there are some things to do right in front of you. (Blank) and (blank) and (blank.) Agreed? Can you tell me something that is more important in the next XX hours? Okay, then. If that changes, let me know. I'm glad we're on the same page."

For yourself, don't feel like you have to seek out instances of doing "the duty of the moment." They will come to you. That attitude of being willing to respond to God's leading will spark daily opportunities to fill the needs of people around us. Your kids will see that. If they don't, you have full permission to share with your family how God used you today.

Don't worry, you will never be expected to do *more* than you can. You are merely expected to do *all* that you can.

Wise decision making requires
...more than just going with your gut.
...more than just knowing man's laws.
...knowledge, experience, and accountability.
...big-picture thinking.

Give parameters

One of the great fears of parents is that when we allow our children to make decisions, they will be bad ones. They will choose shorts and a T-shirt on the coldest day of the year. They will choose gummy bears for dinner. They will choose to watch SpongeBob reruns all day Saturday. Well, what else do you expect when you let them choose what to wear, what to eat, and what to do?

Remind them often who's in charge and insist they eat, wear, and do what you say. But there is a way you can let your kids of any age practice decision making and never make a bad decision. Really. Give them two or three perfectly acceptable options and let them choose their preference.

That's easy when they're in grade school. Moms have been doing this with young girls' outfits for years. But how does it work during the teen years? Instead of choices, give parameters.

"Yes, you can decorate your room. But you can't tear down any walls, paint any woodwork, do any electrical work, or create a dangerous environment."

"Yes, you can go to the mall. But be back by nine p.m., answer your cell phone, and don't even walk into Victoria's Secret."

"Yes, apply to as many colleges as you want. But they should all be within 200 miles of home."

Truthfully, kids like parameters. It gives them a sense of security and actually opens their minds to options within those boundaries. If your son or daughter wants to challenge one of your parameters, that's a good thing. Allow them to respectfully present a reasonable response or argument and then take the time to consider it with care.

"Can I put in a ceiling fan?"

"If we go to a seven o'clock movie, it might be closer to nine-thirty. Is that okay?"

"I've been researching marine biology programs and I might need to go to school out of state."

For their first billion decisions, giving them options and parameters requires only a short discussion. Lengthier and more interesting conversations may occur when they realize that life gives its own set of options and parameters. Things like budgets, weather, calendars, deadlines, geography, height, athletic ability, and overlapping schedules. They're going to find out that they can't do everything they want to do. Closed doors and alternate opportunities can also come from other people, past promises, new information, and directly from God. Sometimes, your child has to make a tough choice.

It can be really hard to watch your child face an insurmountable wall (that is, a parameter) that they just can't climb over. That's when you'll be glad you gave them a lifetime of practice in making decisions.

Weigh both sides

Most decisions have a myriad of options. Your tough-minded son or daughter could join one of five active-duty branches of the U.S. military. Or munch on one of 29 flavors of Pop-Tarts. There were approximately 2.2 million books published this year and you chose to read this one.

But let's say you or your child has narrowed the options down to two. Soup or salad. Fly or drive. Baseball or track. Law or medicine. You may want to try the method described by Benjamin Franklin in a note he wrote to the British scientist Joseph Priestley. Here's an excerpt from a letter dated September 19, 1772:

> To get over this (indecision), my way is to divide half a sheet of paper by a line into two columns; writing over the one Pro, and over the other Con. Then, during three or four days consideration, I put down under the different heads short hints of the different motives, that at different times occur to me, for or against the measure. When I have thus got them all together in one view, I endeavor to estimate their respective weights; and where I find two, one on each side, that seem equal, I strike them both out. If I find a reason pro equal to some two reasons con, I strike out the three. If I judge some two reasons con, equal to some three reasons pro, I strike out the five; and thus

proceeding I find at length where the balance lies; and if, after a day or two of further consideration nothing new that is of importance occurs on either side, I come to a determination accordingly.

Don't encourage your kid to waste 20 minutes of their life and a perfectly good sheet of paper deciding on what Pop-Tart to eat. But creating side-by-side columns as described by old Ben might be a good way to choose between something more significant, like whether to attend your local public high school or the private prep school in the next town.

Let your eighth-grader create the two-column chart and write down the pros and cons. In your gut, you may feel strongly one way or the other. Still, you want to recommend positive comments for both sides. If you're clever enough, you can influence the final decision with persuasive remarks that stack the deck one way or other.

Even if you're subtle, older kids will pick up on what you're trying to do. And that's not a bad thing. They really do want your opinion. Just make sure you consider their comments as well.

Don't say no, say yes

Often, a dad will need to take charge and make a decision to protect our kids. Sometimes the answer should be a firm and decisive "No." But since you and I are just about the nicest guys in the world, we don't want to say that. Which means sometimes we reluctantly say something like, "Okay, but be careful" or "Okay, but just this one time." Even worse, we sometimes hide behind our newspaper or computer screen and pretend we aren't aware that any decision making is going on.

While coaching wrestling, I came across a concept that may help in this area. Instead of saying no to one thing, say yes to something else.

Let me explain. One of the most challenging concepts for young wrestlers is "locked hands." In youth and high school wrestling, when a boy is "on top" his primary goal is to turn his opponent on his back for a pin. Sometimes, though, the wrestler on top finds himself hanging on for dear life simply trying not to lose his advantage by getting "reversed" or allowing his opponent to "escape." One strategy would be to wrap your arm around the other guy's waist and grab your own hand or wrist. Except that's illegal. That's "locked hands" and results in a penalty point.

If you're an old coach, wrestler, or observant parent, you're laughing right now. Teaching young wrestlers not to lock hands is one of the great frustrations for a coach. From the edge of the mat, a coach can say, "Don't lock your hands." But the wrestler just can't help it. Locking hands is instinctive. As soon as those two hands touch, the ref blows the whistle, stops the match, and awards a penalty point. So here's a better plan. Instead of yelling, "Don't lock your hands," give them a proactive command. Suggest something else to do with their hands. That's why you'll hear good coaches call out, "deep waist," "pick an ankle," "break him down," or "grab a wrist." That gives the wrestler something to do besides just hang on. Plus, it may lead to something even better—turning your opponent on his back.

By suggesting something proactive, you prevent the penalty and you advance your cause. You're replacing a negative with a positive. Here are a few off-the-mat examples for dads.

Want to stop smoking? Don't just say no to nicotine, say yes to celery.

Want to stop yelling at referees? Volunteer to keep score, shoot game video, work the concession stand, work the chain gang, or be the ref.

Want to cut down on desserts? Take a walk after dinner.

Want to stop yelling at your kids for being late getting in the car for church Sunday mornings? Serve hot waffles one hour before the service begins.

And a few applications for your kids:

Want them to put down the video game? Toss them a fresh can of tennis balls and send them to the park district courts. (Or join them!)

Want them to stop smoking pot? Take them mountain biking. Or hang gliding. Or find some other high they can get naturally. (With you.)

They don't put their clothes on hangers? Install 20 hooks instead.

Do they whine about dinner? Sign them up to volunteer with you at a soup kitchen.

Make sense? If it does, spend a few minutes right now listing three personal negative habits of your own. Sleep on it. Then tomorrow list three positive replacements.

If it works, tell your kids.

The danger of teeny, tiny bad decisions

I believe one of the greatest dangers in our world today is the slippery slope. Church bingo leads to a state-run lottery, which leads to a plethora of casinos. An innocent flirtation leads to a long lunch, which leads to a marriage-destroying affair. Vulgar language leads to more vulgar language. And so on.

I know you have raised your children to understand the concept of good choices and bad choices. What they don't realize is how easily one teeny, tiny bad choice leads to another. In C.S. Lewis's memorable book *The Screwtape Letters*, the diabolical elder demon pens some wise advice to his apprentice advocating the effectiveness of the slippery slope. Uncle Screwtape writes, "The safest road to Hell is the gradual one. This is the road taken by quiet people, responsible citizens, religious people, our neighbors and even people participating in the Christian church."

J.C. Ryle (1816–1900), the first Anglican bishop of Liverpool, said something profound you may want to share with your children: "They may look small and insignificant, but mind what I say, resist them—make no compromise, let no sin lodge quietly and undisturbed in your heart."

Be warned. When you confront one of your kids about a bad choice they might be making, if your main concern is how it will lead to other bad choices, they'll deny that possibility. "Just because I smoked one cigarette doesn't mean I'm going to start smoking pot or doing cocaine." "Just because I didn't pay for a drink refill doesn't mean I'm going to be a bank robber." "Just because I drove without a seatbelt one time doesn't mean I'm a terrible driver."

Dad, don't get sucked into that argument. Instead, establish that the early choice was wrong all by itself. "Yes, we all make mistakes. And I know you're not a nasty, evil criminal. But we've talked about right and wrong before. Let's stay on the 'good choice' side of life. It's so much easier on your old man. Okay?"

If you can give an example from your own life, then you've got a good chance of being heard. Even if it's remembering a friend or acquaintance from your youth. "There was this girl—in fifth grade—she was boy-crazy. Her name was Anita. By middle school she was dating. And in high school she got pregnant. Twice." "Two starters from our high school basketball team—good kids—went to one beer party and got caught. They rode the bench for a month and lost their college scholarships. All from one bad choice."

Please don't count on the schools

Most public middle schools have a much-heralded program that supposedly teaches "decision-making skills." With the best of intentions, they present some nationally accredited miracle curriculum as an exciting new way to fight gangs, drug abuse, teenage pregnancy, suicide, graffiti, and bullying. Suddenly all the young people in town are going to get along, make impeccable choices, be financially independent, help little old ladies across the street, and keep their shirts tucked in.

But it can't possibly work. Why? Because these programs cannot and will never point to an absolute truth. They offer only empty platitudes about visualizing excellence or choosing positive attitudes. Allegedly the courses challenge kids to be the best they can be. But what are the standards? The workbooks and videos typically quote athletes, actors, and media celebrities. Apparently, if you're on television, you know how to make wise decisions. Of course, these programs cannot point to God or hold up a Bible and say, "This is the standard." Mention the Ten Commandments and the ACLU will swoop in and threaten a lawsuit based on the separation of church and state.

The best advice these programs offer our young people is, "Search your heart and do what you think is best." Yikes! I don't think I want to live in a world in which teenagers are encouraged to follow their own whims and desires.

Now it's possible these programs actually do have a positive impact for some young people. But your kids have someone who will do a much better job establishing moral boundaries than any public school "life skills programs." That's you, Dad.

Equipping them for life without you

This chapter really isn't about teaching your kids how to make good decisions for today. For now, you're there to monitor and rescue them as necessary. This chapter—this book—is really about teaching your kids how to make good decisions for tomorrow. When you're not immediately available.

Good news. You weren't the best person for the job anyway.

God has a three-point plan for guiding your children in all their decisions. And I recommend you equip your kids with that infallible tool sooner rather than later.

1. First, *point out that knowing the characteristics of God is the road to wise decision making.* He is love, so they know love is always the best choice. He is life, so they know life is precious. He is truth, so they should value honesty and integrity. He is Creator, so they should nurture their creative gifts. He is just, so they can trust him with their lives. He is infinite, so they should keep their eyes focused on eternity.

2. Second, *point your children to Jesus as Savior.* When it comes to "decision-making skills," the one decision to follow Christ is the most important choice your son or daughter will ever make.

3. Third, *the ultimate decision-making tool is the leading of the Holy Spirit.* At the Last Supper, Jesus revealed to his disciples that he was going to the Father but would send "another advocate." Imagine their confusion! Another advocate? How could anyone possibly replace Jesus, their

living, breathing, walking friend who had taught them and guided them with such clarity?

Jesus calmed their fears by saying, "Very truly I tell you, it is for your good that I am going away. Unless I go away, the Advocate will not come to you; but if I go, I will send him to you. When he comes, he will prove the world to be in the wrong about sin and righteousness and judgment" (John 16:7-8). As promised, the second chapter of Acts records the coming of the Holy Spirit, and Christians have been blessed by his supernatural guidance ever since.

Dad, before they reach the age of reason, keep making and modeling wise decisions for your kids. As soon as possible though, turn it over to the Father, Son, and Holy Spirit. You may want to stick around as a clarifying force and sounding board, but give your kids plenty of room to practice and hone the skill of decision making. They need to be able to discern right from wrong and better from best. For their first thousand choices, they're going to need you as their safety net.

Questions to Get Them Talking

1. **What's wrong with making a decision by going with your gut?**

   Talking point: Well, actually, that's the goal. The closer you get to God, the better skills you'll have at making good decisions. That still small voice in your head is going to be tuned into God's best for your life.

2. **In act 1 of *Hamlet*, a father tells his son, "This above all: to thine own self be true." Is that good advice?**

   Talking point: Well, that character, Polonius, ends up spying on his son anyway. And, by the way, is later stabbed to death by Hamlet. So his advice may not be the most reliable. On the other hand, if your "thine own self" is truly pursuing God's will, then it might be the right choice.

3. **If all your friends are doing it, does that make it more likely to be a good decision or bad one?**

   Talking point: If you have real friends with real moral standards, then maybe that's a good sign. But if the culture is saying it's a good thing, then maybe that's an indication that you should head a different direction. The Bible says you have been chosen to be different than the culture. "I have chosen you out of the world. That is why the world hates you" (John 15:19).

4. **How do you make a decision?**

   Talking point: As your kids get older, you can certainly remind them about decisions they made when they were little. The toy they begged for, but then never played with. The certain blankie or stuffed animal they needed in order to sleep. The picture book you read a million times. Explain how adults make decisions. And how you now trust them to reason like an adult. After all, 1 Corinthians 13:11 says, "When I was a child, I spoke and thought and reasoned as a child. But when I grew up, I put away childish things" (NLT).

5. **Need help?**

   Talking point: Go ahead and ask this question often. But just to confirm: Kids will often say no when they really do need help. And they might say yes because they're feeling lazy and want you to do it for them.

Conversations to Pursue

- *Often the best and only answer to a decision is to do what Jesus would do.* Did you have a WWJD bracelet or poster? Maybe read the 1896 book that inspired the idea, *In His Steps* by Charles Sheldon.

- *See if you can anticipate some choices your kids will have to make* before they become last-minute decisions. The goal is to get them thinking ahead. That includes book-report topics, after-school activities, summer jobs, mission trips, careers, spring-break excursions, and choosing a college.

- *Are people making fun of you for being a Christian?* Jesus said in the Sermon on the Mount (as paraphrased in *The Message*), "Count yourself blessed every time people put you down or throw you out or speak lies about you to discredit me. What it means is that the truth is too close for comfort and they are uncomfortable. You can be glad when that happens— give a cheer, even!—for though they don't like it, I do! And all heaven applauds" (Matthew 5:12 MSG).

- *Tell your kids about the concept of "Chesterton's Fence."* G.K. Chesterton (1874–1936) lived during a time of great social change, and many limitations established by previous generations were being challenged. Radical reformers would look at an existing prohibition and discard it with little thought. Chesterton's response was, "Don't ever take a fence down until you know the reason it was put up." In other words, before you move ahead with your plan, take a step back. Look at the old plan and really seek to understand its original purpose. Then make your decision. Maybe the old fence should be taken down. Or maybe not.

- *About to make a huge decision?* Maybe you can break it down into pieces. Try it out. Volunteer at a hospital before deciding to pursue a career in medicine.

- *About to make a huge decision?* Go for it. Jump in with both feet. What's the worst that can happen? Failure is one of your best learning tools.

On Eternity

"Children are the hands by which we hold heaven."
Henry Ward Beecher

*"These commandments that I give you today
are to be on your hearts. Impress them on
your children. Talk about them when you sit
at home and when you walk along the road,
when you lie down and when you get up."*
Deuteronomy 6:6-7

There's a good chance that fatherhood was one of the best things that ever happened to your spiritual life.

Forgive me for the following sweeping generalization. Most of the readers of this book probably didn't spend a lot of time during their teenage years thinking about God. If they did, they put him in a box and pulled him out only on Sundays or when they needed a little help with some teenage problem.

Then, of course, as young men move into their twenties, they typically allow (or invite) all kinds of distractions to push God aside. College. Career. Sex. Drugs. Alcohol. Political causes. Alternative lifestyles. Alternative religions. Military service. Art. Music. Money. Power. Or maybe just a touch of rebellion against Mom, Dad, the government, the establishment, or God himself.

Some of those distractions might be considered worthy pursuits.

Some are just unsavory or unhelpful choices. All of them seem to be an effort to fill a universal human void. I agree with Blaise Pascal, the seventeenth-century mathematician and philosopher, who described the void as an abyss, a God-shaped hole in the heart of every man:

> All men seek happiness. This is without exception. Whatever different means they employ, they all tend to this end... There was once in man a true happiness of which there now remain to him only the mark and empty trace, which he in vain tries to fill from all his surroundings, seeking from things absent the help he does not obtain in things present...But these are all inadequate, because the infinite abyss can only be filled by an infinite and immutable Object, that is to say, only by God Himself.[7]

Intentionally or unknowingly, life is spent in an attempt to fill that infinite abyss. But I believe that quest is never in vain. The quest is noble! I say, keep digging and keep seeking! If you dig down to the deepest reality or seek the highest purpose, you'll eventually find the one true God. God is reaching out to all of us, but it's still up to each of us to reach back. The familiar passage from the Gospel of Matthew confirms this: "Ask and it will be given to you; seek and you will find; knock and the door will be opened to you" (Matthew 7:7). The Old Testament encourages us to put our whole heart and soul into the pursuit of truth: "You will find him if you seek him with all your heart and with all your soul" (Deuteronomy 4:29).

So why do so many guys fall short and feel empty? Don't manly men like you and me enjoy the challenge of a good hunt? It could be that when we're young, selfish, and feeling invincible, we get distracted by the ways of the world and don't see that God has bigger and better plans for our lives. Men settle for what seems to give us the most pleasure with the least effort. And besides, we're in no hurry. We think, *If heaven is real, we've got plenty of time before we meet our Maker, right?*

Then kids come along. We look at those innocent little persons and suddenly we are connected to the future like never before. Tomorrow matters. Which means today matters. Which means our decisions matter and we need to stop speculating about truth and actually find it. For the sake of our kids, our wives, and ourselves. And yikes! *What if someday my kid asks me about God, heaven, Jesus, the Holy Spirit, and all that stuff?*

So, Dad. Congratulations. You no longer have the option of taking the easy way out. For the sake of that child you love so much, you need to get your own spiritual act together. That's a good thing. It's a holy quest. Sincerely seeking God's truth and his will pleases him and gives meaning to our lives.

Let's talk about immortality

By my calculations there are four ways that humans can—in a way—live forever.

One, by creating something of lasting value. A significant work of art. A novel that stands the test of time. A scientific breakthrough that changes the way mankind thinks.

Two, by giving so much of yourself that your life impacts another person. And their life impacts another. And their life impacts another.

Three, by having kids. And then making sure those children value family, so they also want to have kids. Etcetera.

Four, by making sure you live for eternity in heaven.

All four are worthy pursuits. If and when your son or daughter expresses a desire to "make a difference," you can easily steer the conversation toward all the ways an individual can impact many lives for many years. Talk about the value and desirability of art, science, humanitarian work, procreation, and so on.

But then make sure they know there's really only one path to eternal life. Jesus said it many times and many ways, but just before he raised Lazarus from the dead, he clearly told Lazarus' sister, Martha, "I am the resurrection and the life. Anyone who believes in me will live, even after dying" (John 11:25 NLT).

Just in case there was any confusion, Jesus later confirmed that he was not just one way, he was the only way. "I am the way and the

truth and the life. No one comes to the Father except through me"
(John 14:6).

Groundwork for heaven

Concepts like death, heaven, hell, old age, illness, cemeteries, nursing homes, and even hospitals can be traumatic for younger kids. Even as adults, we accept the idea that our earthly life will end, but we have no clear image of what heaven is like. After all, "No eye has seen, no ear has heard, and no mind has imagined what God has prepared for those who love him" (1 Corinthians 2:9 NLT). Hollywood can spend millions on special effects for the screen, trying to conjure up what heaven might be like, but no matter what they come up with, they're not even close.

As adult Christians, we also understand the triumphant battle cry, "Death has been swallowed up in victory. Where, O death, is your victory? Where, O death, is your sting?" (1 Corinthians 15:55). We know there is victory over death in a relationship with Jesus Christ. That's something to celebrate. But younger kids can't process that idea right away.

So Dad, ease your preschool and school-age kids into the idea that heaven is a wonderful place and that a loving God has reserved a place for everyone. True, it's a narrow path and sadly there are people you care about who are not heaven-bound, but that's an idea that will keep young kids up at night. So choose your words carefully. Of course, it's a good thing when a teenager or college student stares at the ceiling contemplating their eternal destination. But for kids of any age, I recommend you first establish that God overflows with love and mercy. Soon enough you can speak intentionally about his justice, vengeance, wrath, and righteousness.

To help communicate all these truths, establish your child's bedroom as a place where prayer is comfortable. Tucking in is a great privilege for fathers. You get to dismantle and push away all the crud from the day and talk about what's really important. When they're young, kids will eagerly welcome you into their world and you'll want to encourage that opening for as long as they live under your roof.

Bedtime prayer should be a routine. But the prayer itself is not routine at all. Find a new reason each night to give glory, give thanks, and ask for God's intervention. Tell your child that God knows their every need, but still loves to hear their heartfelt words. And, please don't include any of that "if I should die before I wake" imagery.

Even better than bedtime prayer is incorporating a "knock and pray" strategy into your shared prayer life. Once in a while knock on your son or daughter's bedroom door and say something like, "I need a quiet place to pray. Can I jump in here for about two minutes?" They may look up slightly confused, but their response will probably be, "Umm. I guess so."

Then, do it. Walk in, sit on the edge of their bed, and almost as if they're not there start praying using actual words. Pray for your situation at work, your wife, your other kids, your own stresses, a neighbor, your community, and any other concerns you might have. End with a prayer for your child who is sitting right there with you. Thank them, kiss their forehead, and leave quietly and gracefully. Does that sound impossible? Allow me to give you an example of how that might sound.

"Heavenly Father, thank you for your generosity and love that you keep pouring on our family. I'm humbled and grateful. I'm challenged to serve you as best I can. You know how the media management project at work is stressing me out, Lord, and I need to ask you for some patience and some new direction. If you could guide my work this week, that would be great.

"For my family, Lord, you know Tim is waiting to hear back from those college applications. Help him trust you and make the right choice for next fall. And for Tammy, help me be the husband she needs. What a gift she is to me and our kids. Please, God, continue to bless our marriage. For Mr. Bradley's surgery. For safe travels next week as I head to Pittsburgh. For the election next month. Lord please let your will be done in all these areas.

"Finally, for Emily. You've given her such a tender heart for others and a great sense of humor. Help her just have a great weekend. Thank you, Lord, for loving us so much and that we are part of your family. Thank you for preparing a place for all of us to be united with you for eternity in heaven. I pray this in the name of your son, Jesus. Amen."

Now that wasn't so hard, was it? Your child may have been stunned by the experience. Or maybe it made perfect sense. In any case, that two minutes achieves about a dozen worthy goals. You prayed. You modeled how to pray. You let your son or daughter know that you believe prayer works. You entered their world. You allowed them to enter your world. You let them know that your marriage is strong. You reminded them that other members of the family have concerns that are equal to or greater than theirs. You let them know your schedule. And you presented heaven as a place where love lives and families are reunited. Plus, prayers like that just might help unleash supernatural forces—such as legions of guardian angels—within the walls of that bedroom.

Perhaps best of all, you have earned the right to return in the near future to pray again. Don't be surprised if your kids start looking forward to your spontaneous prayers and even add some of their own. One word of caution: when your child brings up an issue in prayer, that may be a signal they want to have a conversation with you about it. On the other hand, they weren't talking to you. They were talking to God. So, don't rush in to interrupt that moment. If it feels right, go ahead and say, "Amen. Hey, I'm so glad I was here to pray with you. Is that something you want to talk about?"

One other thought. Don't judge their prayer. God doesn't. He welcomes children with an open heart and open arms. If your daughter wants to pray for the neighbor's lost gerbil, that's fantastic. If she prays for a snow day, that's even better. If your son asks God for forgiveness for calling his little brother "butt face," don't laugh. But you can be sure that makes God smile.

Heaven is

...a real place.
...the eternal home for all believers.
...beyond human imagination.
...where we exchange our weak bodies for glorious bodies.

Anticipating heaven

Have you heard this story? Save it for a time when something not-so-good happens in your child's life and they're asking why God would allow such a thing.

Just about a century ago, as the story goes, a missionary couple who had served for a lifetime overseas and sacrificed much were finally coming back to America. As the ocean liner pulls into the New York City harbor, they hear a band and see a crowd of welcomers cheering and even throwing paper streamers. Touched by the show of appreciation, the husband chokes back a tear and says to his wife, "Look what the body of believers has done to welcome us home after our years of service."

At that moment, the couple sees President Teddy Roosevelt strut down the gangplank waving to the excited crowd, and they immediately realize they had jumped to the wrong conclusion. Soon the crowd disperses and the husband and wife are left alone on the pier with their tattered steamer trunk and discouraged hearts. After a moment, the husband looks heavenward and stammers, "Lord, we have freely given our lives to your work. Is it too much to ask that a few well-wishers greet us when we return home?" With that, a voice rings out gently from the skies, saying, "My child, you're not home yet."

Dad, have you ever thought about the idea that "our citizenship is in heaven" (Philippians 3:20) and we're just visiting? If you can get a middle school kid to understand that truth, you are doing them a great service. High school—and life—will bring disappointments, frustrations, and moments of discouragement you may never know about. There will be times when your beautiful child feels too short, too fat, too gangly, too stubby, or too freckly. Ideally, they learn to look in the mirror and say, "You know what? That's really okay." Because it is! Their imperfect bodies will be glorified after our time on earth is done (Romans 8:17).

Knowing your home is in heaven helps put all kinds of frustrations in perspective for our kids. If their best friend or worst enemy has a nicer house, that's not a problem. Your entire family has a mansion waiting in heaven (John 14:2). When the other girl or guy gets picked by the coach, director, or advisor, there's no need to be jealous. After all, your son or daughter is looking forward to a crown of righteousness which is a much bigger honor (2 Timothy 4:8).

Being aware of our eternal destination is good for adults too. It's a reminder not to get too comfortable here. If you're hanging on too tightly to your possessions or worrying too much about your job title, you may want to check your address. An authentic Christian doesn't live on Maple Avenue or Park Street. Your heart and soul have a forever home on a street paved with gold.

Don't go there

It may not be an appealing topic to pursue with your little ones, but your older kids should be exposed to the Bible's descriptions of hell.

> The cowardly, the unbelieving, the vile, the murderers, the sexually immoral, those who practice magic arts, the idolaters and all liars—they will be consigned to the fiery lake of burning sulfur. This is the second death (Revelation 21:8).

> They will throw them into the blazing furnace, where there will be weeping and gnashing of teeth (Matthew 13:42).

I'm not sure whether the burning sulfur and blazing furnace are metaphors or a literal description of hell. I'm also not sure it matters.

As an aside: That's a conversation you'll want to actively pursue with your kids. Even if they don't bring it up, in the back of their heads they're trying to figure out what to do with the stories, images, and lessons they come across in the Bible. You can explain that the Bible includes all kinds of literary devices and genres—history, laws, letters, poetry, parables, symbolism, life principles, and more. That awareness will help them decide how to interpret a passage and apply it to their life.

For example, the stories of Noah's Ark, the parting of the Red Sea, and David slaying Goliath actually happened. Jesus' parable about the

Good Samaritan was a fictional story he told to make a point about helping your neighbor. Heaven might not have gold roads and a crystal sea, but the imagery and symbolism are pretty clear. If you ever find yourself in a conversation with a curious kid about something in the Bible and you don't know the answer, that's a good thing! Do a little research and figure it out—together!

Back to the not-so-pleasant topic of hell. Perhaps even worse than the promise of fire and brimstone is separation from God and his glory.

> They will be punished with eternal destruction, forever separated from the Lord and from his glorious power (2 Thessalonians 1:9 NLT).

Yes, hell is very real. No, you don't want to go there. And helping your family and friends avoid such a place needs to be a top priority.

Your kids have to own it

With your children, I totally recommend you do dinner-table devotions. And bedtime prayers. And the church thing. And Sunday school. And youth group.

These are minimal expectations you can insist upon because you have relentlessly proven you love them and have their best interest in mind. Even when kids drag their feet or don't seem interested, a dedicated dad will make all those things part of your family's life routine. You're laying a foundation that will serve them well—when they least expect it. When a challenging circumstance requires patience, forgiveness, sacrifice, charity, or self-control, they'll remember those lessons learned in those safe, nurturing experiences.

But there's another step that has to happen. Your kids need to own their faith intellectually. They need to be thinking Christians. They need to be able to defend their faith as described in one of my favorite verses: "Always be prepared to give an answer to everyone who asks you to give the reason for the hope that you have. But do this with gentleness and respect" (1 Peter 3:15).

Are you up for it, Dad? Do you want to help your kids become defenders of the faith? Then, let's dig into some questions that require a little logic and deductive reasoning.

Consider the beloved lyrics of a familiar song: "Jesus loves me! This I know, for the Bible tells me so." As they get older, your sharp kids might say, "Wait a second! How can I know the Bible is even true?" That's an excellent question.

Consider also the well-known passage, "All Scripture is inspired by God and profitable for teaching, for reproof, for correction, for training in righteousness" (2 Timothy 3:16 NASB). A lazy Bible teacher might point to that verse as proof that the Bible is true. But if your son or daughter ends up in a college philosophy class, a liberal professor would easily argue, "That verse doesn't prove anything. It's a classic case of circular logic. That's the Bible claiming that the Bible is true and relevant."

When challenged by an outsider—or by their own curious mind—how will your son or daughter respond? If they ask for your insight and opinion, how will you respond?

Dad, you have to get there first. You don't have to be a Bible historian, archaeologist, or pastor to uncover solid evidence supporting the reliability of the Scriptures. But you will want to dig into the footnotes in your study Bible or peruse some apologetic texts until you have a few "aha!" moments of your own. I recommend books like *More Than a Carpenter* by Josh McDowell, *Foundation* by James L. Nicodem, and *A Case for Christ* by Lee Strobel. I also recommend being part of a men's small group where you can kick around ideas like this.

With just a little effort, you'll discover that the Bible does prove itself to be infallible and reliable over and over again. Here are a few "aha!" moments that struck me as solid, indisputable proof that a Creator God loved me so much that he sent his Son to die on a cross to pay the price for my sins so I could be with him in heaven for eternity.

Prophecies of the Messiah. Historians agree that the Old Testament was written centuries before Jesus arrived. But there are literally hundreds of prophecies in the Old Testament that point very specifically to where, when, and how Jesus would be born, live, die, and rise from the dead. For instance, 700 years before Christ, Micah 5:2 predicts the Messiah will be born in a tiny, little-known town called Bethlehem. Passages in Isaiah predict the virgin birth, Jesus' miracles, and exact circumstances of his crucifixion and burial.

Ongoing archaeological discoveries. Every generation, secular scientists are stunned to uncover new evidence supporting the biblical record, while Christians stand by saying, "We knew it all along." In 1947, a Bedouin goat herder came upon a cave containing jars filled with ancient manuscripts. The so-named Dead Sea Scrolls have confirmed the accuracy of much of today's Old Testament. As another example, for centuries, critics suggested that Old Testament cities such as Petra, Ubar, and Ebla were merely myths. But modern technology and determined archaeologists found them buried in the desert sand. And the list of examples goes on.

The martyrdom of the apostles. History confirms that some 2000 years ago a man named Jesus spent three years teaching in and around present-day Israel, made some friends and some enemies, and was crucified and buried. The real controversy is that he claimed he would rise from the dead. How do we know Jesus was resurrected? I've read many proofs, but let me share just one. The 12 apostles (and many others) saw Jesus alive after the crucifixion!

Could they have been lying? Yes, I suppose. Except that 11 of them died brutal deaths as martyrs because they insisted that Jesus did, in fact, walk on earth for 40 days after that first Easter. Why would these men die for a lie? They wouldn't! If Jesus had died on the cross and stayed buried in the tomb, those men would have scattered, and the entire Christian faith would have ended then and there. Next year, Dad, when you're dyeing Easter eggs as a family, considering sharing this proof— you just might be turning your kids into curious little apologists.

Personal application. I have not yet found a biblical principle that didn't work. Some Old Testament cultural mandates don't apply anymore. But who can deny the thousands of scriptural mandates that create an invaluable formula for life: "Thou shalt not lie." "Flee sexual immorality." "The love of money is the root of all evil." "Work six days, take the seventh day off." "Those who exalt themselves will be humbled." It's more than common sense; it's inspired. On a very personal level, I am continuously aware of the Holy Spirit guiding me in almost all my life decisions…even when I don't ask. Usually, I listen. Regretfully, sometimes I don't.

Those are just four of the foundational principles that have brought me to the faith that guides me today. Still, it goes so much deeper than that. God has generously given me something I can trust. A way of life that gives me a reason to get up in the morning. A narrow path to follow, but one that keeps me safe as I walk in his provision and care. To any dad reading this book, I pray for that same awareness of God's leading for you. I also pray that you experience your own "aha!" moments and share them with your kids. And I pray for wisdom and courage as you help your children discover their own sense of purpose and hope. Isn't that why you picked up this book?

Nothing fancy

I agree with you and most of the world. Sometimes parts of the Bible are hard to understand. There's a quip by Mark Twain that makes me smile and helps me deal with that idea:

> It ain't those parts of the Bible that I can't understand that bother me, it is the parts that I do understand.

Let me share the essence of what I think Mr. Twain is saying. The Bible holds simple truths that you cannot deny—even if there are some things that you don't currently agree with or understand.

With that in mind, don't let your kids be distracted by the bloody battles, weird rules in Leviticus, confusing names, and sheer size of the book itself. Encourage them to dig in. Every verse is there for a reason. The Bible can stand up to scrutiny. But in the end, you and every member of your family have a decision to make. Do you agree or disagree with the following straightforward statement?

Nobody's perfect. We're all sinners. Because of that we're not worthy to hang out with God. Death is inevitable. When I die somebody has to pay for my sin. If it's me, I guess I am going to hell just as I deserve. Thankfully, there's a way out. God sent his only son to live on earth and pay the price for my sins (and yours) on the cross. Best of all, that ticket to heaven cost me nothing. (Same for you.) I just have to understand it and accept that gift.

I'm thinking that Mark Twain was a smart, well-read guy. He understood all this too. I'm hoping that he took a moment from his brilliant wordsmithing to say no to sin and yes to Christ.

Just a taste of heaven on earth

We've already established that there's no way to describe heaven in earthly terms. But there is a way we can find a giant dose of contentment while we're here. The Bible says God and eternity are beyond our understanding. But it also says there is a way God can provide us with a peace that is also beyond our understanding.

> Do not be anxious about anything, but in every situation, by prayer and petition, with thanksgiving, present your requests to God. And the peace of God, which transcends all understanding, will guard your hearts and your minds in Christ Jesus (Philippians 4:6-7).

The peace that comes from God is a taste of heaven. Share it with your kids. Because in the coming years they will experience some anxious moments, they will forget to be thankful, they will try to do things on their own, and their hearts will be broken and their minds confused.

When they need it most, wouldn't it be great if this verse came to mind? Dad, I'm glad you're around to share it.

Questions to Get Them Talking

1. **Do you ever wonder about heaven?**
   Talking point: Don't scare your kids with the idea of death. Instead, ease them into those kinds of conversations. Say

things like, "I don't plan on dying anytime soon. And I'm glad about that. I'm looking forward to seeing all you kids grow up, find someone wonderful to marry, and then make me a grand-father. No hurry, though! I also know you kids need me. I like that. But really, I'm ready for heaven. I'm looking forward to it. And I know God's timing—like always—will be perfect."

2. **Will our dog, cat, gerbil, and turtle be in heaven?**

    Talking point: Here's one way to answer that question. "I don't know. Scripture isn't clear. But, it does say that 'there will be no more death or mourning or crying or pain' (Revelation 21:4). So, I guess that means if missing your pet makes you sad, then Rover, Tiger, Fluffernut, and Slowpoke will all be there. Besides, there were animals in the Garden of Eden, and that was a lot like heaven."

3. **Does becoming a Christian mean all your problems go away?**

    Talking point: Nope—sorry. As a matter of fact, the Bible actually promises that we are going to suffer for our faith. But, don't worry, that only makes us stronger.

    After you have suffered for a little while, the God of all grace, who called you to His eternal glory in Christ, will Himself perfect, confirm, strengthen and establish you (1 Peter 5:10 NASB).

4. **Daddy, how do I become a Christian?**

    Talking point: Don't be scared of that question. Be glad! Be ready! Say, "I've been hoping you'd ask! And you can take care of that right now. It doesn't cost you anything. It's really about understanding, deciding, and praying. You have to understand who God is, who Jesus is, and what sin is. God loves you and wants you to be with him forever. But sin cuts us off from him. Every person who ever lived (except Jesus) has sin in their life. You have to choose to believe that Jesus is God's Son and he died on the cross to pay the penalty for your sins. And then because he rose from the dead, you can also trust him with your life. That prayer is something you can say right now.

"If anything doesn't make sense, please ask me. But if you can, pray these words to God out loud right after me: 'Dear God, I want to know you personally. But my sin gets in the way. My sin even would keep me from being with you forever in heaven. I know that someone has to be punished for that sin, and it should be me. But because you love me, you have provided a way out. You sent your Son, Jesus, who never sinned, to die on the cross and pay the penalty in my place. I know that gift is free to me, but cost Jesus his life. I accept that gift. God, I choose right now to become your child. And I pray from this day forward that you will guide my life and give me a new desire to follow Jesus closely. Thank you for loving me. Amen.'"

Conversations to Pursue

- *As a family, are you so busy with daily life* that you have zero time to stop and consider your place in eternity? This life is a finger snap compared to forever. More important than the next deadline or event on your full family calendar is our relationship with God. Eternity is a line that goes on for… well……eternity!

- *You may have already taught your kids that—in the scope of eternity—"the wages of sin is death"* (Romans 6:23). Shouldn't they also be made aware of the consequences of sin here on earth? Finding forgiveness for sin and following Christ set us free to enjoy his unlimited, unconditional love. Following God doesn't guarantee an easy life, but it does help them live their best life. Both here and in the hereafter.

- *If your kids hide their faith, they never have to defend it.* But if they let friends, classmates, and teammates know they are

Christians, they are going to get a reaction. Some people they meet might say, "Hey, me too!" Some will be envious. Some will be curious. And some will ridicule. Dad, let your kids know about those different responses before they come. And maybe even talk through how they might respond.

- *Specifically, how would you suggest* your son or daughter respond to statements like these? "Church is for people who can't think for themselves," "Religion is all just a bunch of rules," or "I tried church. Boring!"

- *You or your kids may sometimes wonder if they are saved.* Charles Colson said, "If Christ's lordship does not disrupt our lordship, then the reality of our conversion must be questioned." The Bible suggests a few tests.

  Check your actions. Do they follow God's laws? "Whoever says, 'I know him,' but does not do what he commands is a liar, and the truth is not in that person. But if anyone obeys his word, love for God is truly made complete in them" (1 John 2:4-5).

  Check your "guilt level." Are you convicted each time you sin? "If you are not disciplined—and everyone undergoes discipline—then you are not legitimate, not true sons and daughters at all" (Hebrews 12:8).

  Check your hunger for the Bible. Does it speak right to your heart? "The law from your mouth is more precious to me than thousands of pieces of silver and gold" (Psalm 119:72).

- *You only have to receive Christ once.* It's common for younger children to say the "Sinner's Prayer" several times over a few months, just to make sure. That's not a huge problem. But they should know that once they've truly surrendered their life to Christ, they can be confident in their faith. They have been fully justified. That's a one-time deal. The process of sanctification—growing in Christ and becoming more like him—goes on until your last day on earth.

Ending Conversations

Much of this book is devoted to launching conversations. Entering your child's world. Breaking the ice. Asking thought-provoking questions. Fanning the flames of curiosity in your children. Tackling the tough topics. And encouraging your kids to come to you routinely with good news, bad news, an amusing anecdote, or a personal challenge.

But perhaps even more important than *launching* conversations is *finishing them* wisely and well. Not every dialogue has to be a five-star, life-changing elocutionary masterpiece. Don't expect your son or daughter to punctuate every conversation by saying, "Thanks for your inspired wisdom and advice, Father." But you will want to make sure any talks you have usually end on a high note.

Specifically, ask yourself if your time together was spent talking to each other or past each other. Did teen slang, indecipherable texts, morning mumbles, loud music, or earbuds prevent any real communication from actually taking place? Was zero information traded? Or too much information expressed in too little time?

As the parent, we often have to take a stand. There's always the risk, however, that you might "win" the argument, but come out feeling like you lost a small part of your relationship with that child you care so much about.

Redeeming abrupt endings

Realistically, you should expect an occasional conversation with your son or daughter to end less than blissfully. They may give in to your parental authority but exhale a final one- or two-word mutter.

"Fine." "You win." "Whatever."

Don't gloat. Don't celebrate the conquest as if you and your child are enemies. Remind yourself that you're on the same team. Take a moment to consider how next time you might be able to resolve the conflict in such a way that both of you can claim victory. Could you have been clearer about expectations? In the future, can you give them a little more advance warning? Were you listening when they told you about the plans they had made months ago?

As the parent, you have the right to make the final decision. You have the right to say, "No." But last minute "No's" with zero explanation are hard to take.

Some dads experience even more difficult endings to conversations than short mutterings. Maybe you've witnessed a child you desperately love storm out of a room with a spite-filled rant that pierces your heart.

"That's ridiculous." "You have no idea what you're talking about." "I hate this family."

Dad, conversations cannot end this way. Your first instinct might be to lash back, but you know that's the wrong response. Also, don't give in to wishful thinking that the matter will take care of itself. Don't wait a week. Don't wait until tomorrow. It may sound close to impossible, but the best idea might be to take a breath, try to feel their pain, gather your thoughts, and in a matter of minutes knock gently on their door and call their name.

Behind that door, they're angry. No doubt. But they're also regretting their harsh words. If you can avoid pushing their buttons, you might be able to defuse the entire episode before it escalates into a monthlong wasteland of anger, resentment, and brokenness. The goal is to say something that acknowledges their frustration but also reinforces your role as shepherd, authority, and voice of reason. Be aware. It might be a very short and mostly one-sided conversation.

"Angela, it breaks my heart that you're hurting this much."

"Michael, I know this didn't turn out the way you wanted. And there are very likely things you're dealing with that I'm not even aware of. But your mother and I made this decision with a lot of thought and I'm asking you to trust us."

"Son, I need your help. I need you to listen to me for just a few more seconds. Conversations can't end like this. We're in this together. And I need you to know that I love you and sometimes I make mistakes. But I will always do what I think is best for you and every member of this family."

"We'll get through this. I promise. Let me know if you want to talk. But if you don't, that's fine. I get it."

There are no magic words here. But there needs to be a sense that you are as broken as they are. You really do care about how they feel and what they think. Whatever has transpired, you have chosen to forge ahead with a calm and quiet strength. There's work to be done and you're still in charge. No matter what, Dad, your kids want and need you to be strong.

Think of it this way. You will have thousands of conversations with each of your kids. At the end of just about every one, you want to be pulling your child toward you. Not pushing them away.

The end of the Gospels

The relationship you're building with your growing children will continue long after they leave home. But each individual conversation still requires an ending. Let's consider for a moment how God inspired Matthew, Mark, Luke, and John to close off each of the Gospels.

Matthew ends with Jesus' clear command, often referred to as the "Great Commission."

> Go and make disciples of all nations, baptizing them in the name of the Father and of the Son and of the Holy Spirit,

and teaching them to obey everything I have commanded you. And surely I am with you always, to the very end of the age (Matthew 28:19-20).

Mark takes those marching orders a step further, describing the actual actions performed by the disciples.

After the Lord Jesus had spoken to them, he was taken up into heaven and he sat at the right hand of God. Then the disciples went out and preached everywhere, and the Lord worked with them and confirmed his word by the signs that accompanied it (Mark 16:19-20).

Luke crams quite a bit of action into the last few verses of the Gospel he penned. He describes a gathering, a blessing, some worship, and joyful praise.

When [Jesus] had led them out to the vicinity of Bethany, he lifted up his hands and blessed them. While he was blessing them, he left them and was taken up into heaven. Then they worshiped him and returned to Jerusalem with great joy. And they stayed continually at the temple, praising God (Luke 24:50-53).

John's Gospel ends with a bit of a mystery. It's an open-ended invitation to imagine the life of Jesus. The fullness of what he did and who he was can't be written down or ignored. It's too big. Too magnificent.

Jesus did many other things as well. If every one of them were written down, I suppose that even the whole world would not have room for the books that would be written (John 21:25).

That's four pretty solid choices when it comes to ending conversations. Give specific instructions. Do something worth doing. Bless your children by pointing them to God. Give them something wonderful to think about so they can make their own decisions long after you're gone.

If you haven't realized it yet, allow me to remind you. The whole purpose of conversations with your children while they are under your roof is to successfully get them out on their own. In a sense, to talk your way out of a job.

Years from now, when they need it most, they'll remember your words, your wisdom, and the way you lived your life.

> *"Life is no brief candle to me. It is a sort of splendid torch which I have got a hold of for the moment, and I want to make it burn as brightly as possible before handing it on to future generations."*
>
> George Bernard Shaw

Notes

1. Darby E. Southgate, Vincent J. Roscigno, "The Impact of Music on Childhood and Adolescent Achievement," http://johnroscigno-conductor.yolasite.com/resources/Impact%20of%20 Music%20on%20Youth%20Article%20by%20V.%20Roscigno.pdf.

2. *IU News Room*, "Divorce begets divorce but not genetically" (Indiana University press release), http://newsinfo.iu.edu/news-archive/5982.html.

3. W. Bradford Wilcox, "Is Religion an Answer? Marriage, Fatherhood, and the Male Problematic," The Center for Marriage and Families, *Research Brief No. 11*, June 2008.

4. Vaughn R.A. Call and Tim B. Heaton, "Religious Influence on Marital Stability," *Journal for the Scientific Study of Religion* 36, no. 3 (September 1997): pp. 382-392.

5. James Trussell, "Contraceptive efficacy," in R.A. Hatcher et al., *Contraceptive Technology*, 20th ed. (New York: Ardent Media, 2011), pp. 779-863, retrieved online 2011-03-13.

6. Anthony Paik, "Adolescent Sexuality and Risk of Marital Dissolution," *Journal of Marriage and Family* 73 (2011): pp. 483-484.

7. Blaise Pascal, *Pensées* 425 (Section VII, "Morality and Doctrine").

Material adapted from other Harvest House Publishers books by Jay Payleitner:

Conversation 1: The Rae Anne/Rachel story is from *52 Things Daughters Need from Their Dad* (2013), chapter 1.

Conversation 2: The chalk-talk story is from *52 Things Sons Need from Their Dad* (2014), chapter 11. The section about teaching kids concepts years ahead of time is from Payleitner, *52 Things Kids Need from a Dad* (2010), chapter 44.

Conversation 4: The new garage-door story is from *52 Things Kids Need*, chapter 15.

Conversation 5: The section about the author's career path is from *52 Things Sons Need*, chapter 36. Material under the subheading "Their first job" is from *52 Things Daughters Need*, chapter 39.

Conversation 6: The bullet points with money advice are from Payleitner, *52 Things Wives Need from Their Husband* (2012), chapter 17. The "this is now your money" story is from *One-Minute Devotions for Dads* (2012), "Financial Acumen 101" chapter.

Conversation 10: The "knock and pray" story is from *52 Things Daughters Need*, chapter 24.

Books by Jay Payleitner

Once Upon a Tandem

The One Year Life Verse Devotional

52 Things Kids Need from a Dad

365 Ways to Say "I Love You" to Your Kids

52 Things Wives Need from Their Husbands

One-Minute Devotions for Dads

If God Gave Your Graduation Speech

52 Things Daughters Need from Their Dads

52 Things Husbands Need from Their Wives

If God Wrote Your Birthday Card

52 Things Sons Need from Their Dad

About the author

Jay Payleitner is a dad. But he pays his mortgage and feeds his family working as a freelance writer, ad man, motivational speaker, and radio producer with credits including *Josh McDowell Radio, WordPower, Jesus Freaks Radio,* and *Today's Father with Carey Casey.* Jay served as the Executive Director for the Illinois Fatherhood Initiative and is a featured writer/ blogger for the National Center for Fathering. He is the author of the bestselling *52 Things Kids Need from a Dad, 365 Ways to Say "I Love You" to Your Kids,* and *The One-Year Life Verse Devotional.* He is also creator of "The Dad Manifesto." Jay and his high school sweetheart, Rita, have four sons, one daughter, and four daughters-in-law and live in St. Charles, Illinois. You can read his weekly dadblog at jaypayleitner.com.

National Center for Fathering

Engaging fathers. Enriching lives.

The National Center for Fathering (NCF) is a nonprofit 501(c)(3) organization created in 1990 in response to the incredible social and economic impact of fatherlessness in America.

At the National Center for Fathering, we work to improve the lives of children and reverse the trends of fatherlessness by inspiring and equipping fathers, grandfathers, and father figures to be actively engaged in the life of *every* child.

We focus our work in four key areas:

Research. At the core of all the National Center's work is the Championship Fathering Profile. Developed by a team of researchers led by NCF's founder, Ken R. Canfield, PhD, this assessment tool helps men understand their strengths and opportunities as a father. NCF continues to partner with researchers and practitioners interested in expanding the knowledge base of the fathering field.

Training. NCF offers training through seminars, small groups, and training programs. We have reached over 80,000 fathers through our seminars and have equipped more than 1000 trainers to provide our research-based father training in their local communities.

Programs. NCF provides impactful and meaningful fathering programs that enrich the lives of fathers, children, and families. WATCH D.O.G.S. (Dads Of Great Students), our flagship program, is currently in 46 states, four countries, and more than 4000 schools. WATCH D.O.G.S. is a one-of-a-kind school-based father-involvement program that works to support education and safety.

Resources. Our website provides a wealth of free resources for dads in nearly every fathering situation, including new dads and granddads, divorced dads and stepfathers, adoptive dads and father figures. Dads who join our *Championship Fathering Team* receive a weekly e-mail full of timely and practical tips on fathering. We also have a daily radio program that features Carey Casey, our CEO, and airs on 350-plus stations. Listen to programs online or download podcasts at fathers.com/radio.

For more information, please visit www.fathers.com.

Make your commitment to Championship Fathering

Championship Fathering is an effort to change the culture for today's children and the children of coming generations. We're seeking to reach, teach, and unleash 6.5 million dads, creating a national movement of men who will commit to LOVE their children, COACH their children, MODEL for their children, ENCOURAGE other children, and ENLIST other dads to join the team. To make the Championship Fathering commitment, visit fathers.com/cf.

Also by Jay Payleitner

52 Things Sons Need from Their Dads
What Fathers Can Do to Build a Lasting Relationship

Bestselling author Jay Payleitner, dad of four grown sons, gives you a bucketful of man-friendly ideas on building a father-son relationship that will last into eternity. By your life, your example, and a few well-chosen words you can...

- show your boy why it's good to be a guy
- demonstrate how to treat women well
- teach him to work hard, set lofty goals, and find joy in the quest
- generate a positive outcome from competition, digital media, and video games
- lead him to count on God for the strength and confidence to live a purposeful life

Jay's 52 quick-to-read chapters offer real-life strategies that will inspire you and your son to keep fighting the good fight—together and on the same side!

365 Ways to Say "I Love You" to Your Kids

Expressions of love can get lost in the crush of carpools, diaper changes, homework, and afterschool activities. But Jay Payleitner is here to help you turn the dizzying array of activities into great memories. Learn to say "I love you"...

> ...at bedtime...in the car...in different languages...without words...doing chores... when your kids mess up big time...on vacation...using secret phrases...in crazy unexpected ways...in everyday life...in ways that point to God.

Whether your kids are newborn or college-bound, these 365 simple suggestions—from silly to serious—will help you lead your precious pack to joy, laughter, and connection one "I love you" at a time.

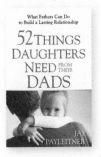

52 Things Daughters Need from Their Dads
What Fathers Can Do to Build a Lasting Relationship

The days of tea parties, stuffed doggies, and butterfly kisses are oh-so-important, but they don't last forever. So how can a dad safeguard his daughter so she grows up strong, healthy, beautiful, and confident?

Jay Payleitner has given valuable, man-friendly advice to thousands of dads in his bestselling *52 Things Kids Need from a Dad*. Now Jay guides you into what may be unexplored territory—*girl land*—and gives you ways to...

- date your daughter
- be on the lookout for "hero moments" and make lasting memories
- protect her from eating disorders and other cultural curses
- scare off the scoundrels and welcome the young men who might be worthy
- give your daughter a positive view of men

Jay will help you feel encouraged with 52 creative ideas to give you confidence in relating to your precious daughter...in ways that will help her blossom into the woman God has designed her to be.

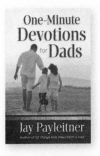

One-Minute Devotions for Dads

Lots of dads feel a twinge of terror at the word *devotion*. Something dull and guilt-producing. Something you're supposed to read at 5 a.m. before you do your 100 push-ups and eat your bowl of oat bran.

Enter Jay Payleitner, exit terror. A veteran dad, Jay knows how regular guys think because he is one. His Bible-based coaching sessions—devotions, if you must—offer you unexpected but relevant thoughts and touches of offbeat humor. And "What About You?" wrap-ups leave you with something straightforward to do or think about.

Young dads, older dads—your day will get a shot in the arm from Jay's seasoned wisdom and God-centered thinking.

To learn more about Harvest House books and
to read sample chapters, visit our website:

www.harvesthousepublishers.com

HARVEST HOUSE PUBLISHERS
EUGENE, OREGON